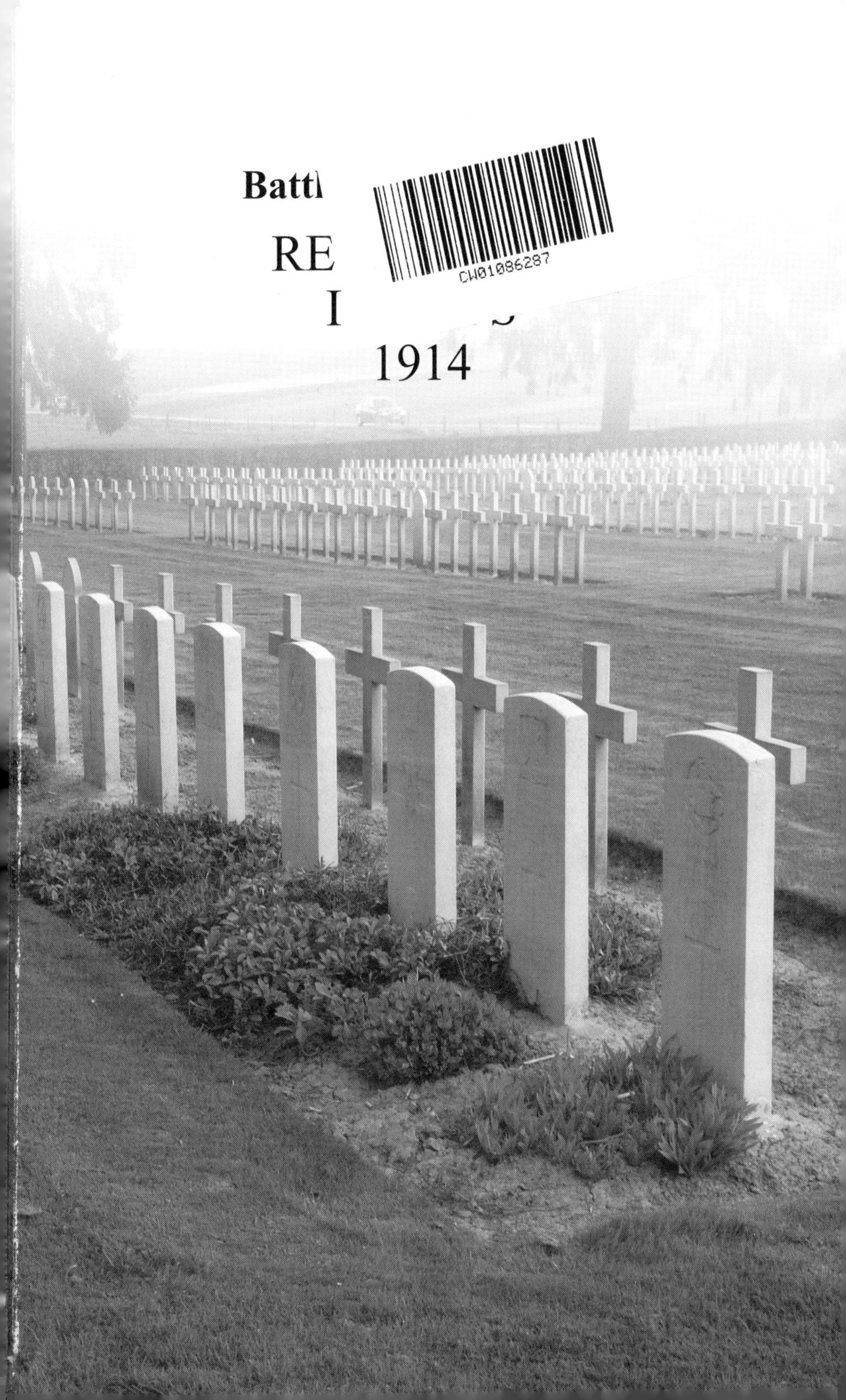
Battl
RE
I
1914
CW01086287

Battleground series:

Stamford Bridge & Hastings *by* Peter Marren
***Wars of the Roses* - Wakefield/ Towton** *by* Philip A. Haigh
***Wars of the Roses* - Barnet** *by* David Clark
***Wars of the Roses* - Tewkesbury** *by* Steven Goodchild
***Wars of the Roses* - The Battles of St Albans** *by* Peter Burley, Michael Elliott & Harvey Wilson
***English Civil War* - Naseby** *by* Martin Marix Evans, Peter Burton and Michael Westaway
***English Civil War* - Marston Moor** *by* David Clark
***War of the Spanish Succession* - Blenheim 1704** *by* James Falkner
***War of the Spanish Succession* - Ramillies 1706** *by* James Falkner
***Napoleonic* - Hougoumont** *by* Julian Paget and Derek Saunders
***Napoleonic* - Waterloo** *by* Andrew Uffindell and Michael Corum
***Zulu War* - Isandlwana** *by* Ian Knight and Ian Castle
***Zulu War* - Rorkes Drift** *by* Ian Knight and Ian Castle
***Boer War* - The Relief of Ladysmith** *by* Lewis Childs
***Boer War* - The Siege of Ladysmith** *by* Lewis Childs
***Boer War* - Kimberley** *by* Lewis Childs

Mons *by* Jack Horsfall and Nigel Cave
Néry *by* Patrick Tackle
Le Cateau *by* Nigel Cave and Jack Shelden
Walking the Salient *by* Paul Reed
Ypres, 1914: Langemarck *by* Jack Sheldon and Nigel Cave
Ypres, 1914: Messines *by* Jack Sheldon and Nigel Cave
Ypres, 1914: The Menin Road *by* Nigel Cave and Jack Sheldon
***Ypres* - Sanctuary Wood and Hooge** *by* Nigel Cave
***Ypres* - Hill 60** *by* Nigel Cave
***Ypres* - Messines Ridge** *by* Peter Oldham
***Ypres* - Polygon Wood** *by* Nigel Cave
***Ypres* - Passchendaele** *by* Nigel Cave
***Ypres* - Airfields and Airmen** *by* Mike O'Connor
***Ypres* - St Julien** *by* Graham Keech
Walking the Somme *by* Paul Reed
***Somme* - Gommecourt** *by* Nigel Cave
***Somme* - Serre** *by* Jack Horsfall & Nigel Cave
***Somme* - Beaumont Hamel** *by* Nigel Cave
***Somme* - Thiepval** *by* Michael Stedman
***Somme* - La Boisselle** *by* Michael Stedman
***Somme* - Fricourt** *by* Michael Stedman
***Somme* - Carnoy-Montauban** *by* Graham Maddocks
***Somme* - Pozières** *by* Graham Keech
***Somme* - Courcelette** *by* Paul Reed
***Somme* - Boom Ravine** *by* Trevor Pidgeon
***Somme* - Mametz Wood** *by* Michael Renshaw
***Somme* - Delville Wood** *by* Nigel Cave
***Somme* - Advance to Victory (North) 1918** *by* Michael Stedman
Somme - Flers *by* Trevor Pidgeon
***Somme* - Bazentin Ridge** *by* Edward Hancock
***Somme* - Combles** *by* Paul Reed
***Somme* - Beaucourt** *by* Michael Renshaw
***Somme* - Redan Ridge** *by* Michael Renshaw
***Somme* - Hamel** *by* Peter Pedersen
***Somme* - Villers-Bretonneux** *by* Peter Pedersen
***Somme* - Airfields and Airmen** *by* Mike O'Connor
Airfields and Airmen of the Channel Coast *by* Mike O'Connor
In the Footsteps of the Red Baron *by* Mike O'Connor
***Arras* - Airfields and Airmen** *by* Mike O'Connor
***Arras* - The Battle for Vimy Ridge** *by* Jack Sheldon & Nigel Cave
***Arras* - Vimy Ridge** *by* Nigel Cave
***Arras* - Gavrelle** *by* Trevor Tasker and Kyle Tallett
***Arras* - Oppy Wood** *by* David Bilton
***Arras* - Bullecourt** *by* Graham Keech
***Arras* - Monchy le Preux** *by* Colin Fox
Walking Arras *by* Paul Reed
Hindenburg Line *by* Peter Oldham
***Hindenburg Line* - Epehy** *by* Bill Mitchinson
***Hindenburg Line* - Riqueval** *by* Bill Mitchinson
***Hindenburg Line* - Villers-Plouich** *by* Bill Mitchinson
***Hindenburg Line* - Cambrai Right Hook** *by* Jack Horsfall & Nigel Cave
***Hindenburg Line* - Cambrai Flesquières** *by* Jack Horsfall & Nigel Cave
***Hindenburg Line* - Saint Quentin** *by* Helen McPhail and Philip Guest
***Hindenburg Line* - Bourlon Wood** *by* Jack Horsfall & Nigel Cave
***Cambrai* - Airfields and Airmen** *by* Mike O'Connor
Aubers Ridge *by* Edward Hancock
***La Bassée* - Neuve Chapelle** *by* Geoffrey Bridger
***Loos* - Hohenzollern Redoubt** *by* Andrew Rawson
***Loos* - Hill 70** *by* Andrew Rawson
Fromelles *by* Peter Pedersen
Accrington Pals Trail *by* William Turner
Poets at War: Wilfred Owen *by* Helen McPhail and Philip Guest
Poets at War: Edmund Blunden *by* Helen McPhail and Philip Guest
Poets at War: Graves & Sassoon *by* Helen McPhail and Philip Guest
Gallipoli *by* Nigel Steel
***Gallipoli* - Gully Ravine** *by* Stephen Chambers
***Gallipoli* - Anzac, The Landing** *by* Stephen Chambers
***Gallipoli* - Landings at Helles** *by* Huw & Jill Rodge
Walking the Italian Front *by* Francis Mackay
***Italy* - Asiago** *by* Francis Mackay
***Verdun:* Fort Douamont** *by* Christina Holstein
Zeebrugge & Ostend Raids 1918 *by* Stephen McGreal

Germans at Beaumont Hamel *by* Jack Sheldon
Germans at Thiepval *by* Jack Sheldon

SECOND WORLD WAR

Dunkirk *by* Patrick Wilson
Calais *by* Jon Cooksey
Boulogne *by* Jon Cooksey
Saint-Nazaire *by* James Dorrian
***Normandy* - Pegasus Bridge/Merville Battery** *by* Carl Shilleto
***Normandy* - Utah Beach** *by* Carl Shilleto
***Normandy* - Omaha Beach** *by* Tim Kilvert-Jones
***Normandy* - Gold Beach** *by* Christopher Dunphie & Garry Johnson
***Normandy* - Gold Beach Jig** *by* Tim Saunders
***Normandy* - Juno Beach** *by* Tim Saunders
***Normandy* - Sword Beach** *by* Tim Kilvert-Jones
***Normandy* - Operation Bluecoat** *by* Ian Daglish
***Normandy* - Operation Goodwood** *by* Ian Daglish
***Normandy* - Epsom** *by* Tim Saunders
***Normandy* - Hill 112** *by* Tim Saunders
***Normandy* - Mont Pinçon** *by* Eric Hunt
***Normandy* - Cherbourg** *by* Andrew Rawson
***Das Reich* – Drive to Normandy** *by* Philip Vickers
Oradour *by* Philip Beck
***Market Garden* - Nijmegen** *by* Tim Saunders
***Market Garden* - Hell's Highway** *by* Tim Saunders
***Market Garden* - Arnhem, Oosterbeek** *by* Frank Steer
***Market Garden* - Arnhem, The Bridge** *by* Frank Steer
***Market Garden* - The Island** *by* Tim Saunders
Rhine Crossing – US 9th Army & 17th US Airborne *by* Andrew Rawson
British Rhine Crossing – Operation Varsity *by* Tim Saunders
British Rhine Crossing – Operation Plunder *by* Tim Saunders
***Battle of the Bulge* – St Vith** *by* Michael Tolhurst
***Battle of the Bulge* – Bastogne** *by* Michael Tolhurst
Channel Islands *by* George Forty
Walcheren *by* Andrew Rawson
Remagen Bridge *by* Andrew Rawson
Cassino *by* Ian Blackwell
Anzio *by* Ian Blackwell
Dieppe *by* Tim Saunders
Fort Eben Emael *by* Tim Saunders
***Crete* – Operation 'Merkur'** *by* Tim Saunders

Battleground Europe

RETREAT OF I CORPS 1914

Jerry Murland

Series Editor
Nigel Cave

Pen & Sword
MILITARY

First published in Great Britain in 2014 by
Pen & Sword Military
An imprint of
Pen & Sword Books Ltd
47 Church Street
Barnsley
South Yorkshire
S70 2AS

Copyright © Jerry Murland, 2014

ISBN 978 178346 373 2

The right of Jerry Murland to be identified as Author
of this work has been asserted by him in accordance with the
Copyright, Designs and Patents Act 1988.

A CIP catalogue record for this book is
available from the British Library.

All rights reserved. No part of this book may be reproduced or
transmitted in any form or by any means, electronic or mechanical
including photocopying, recording or by any information storage and retrieval
system, without permission from the Publisher in writing.

Typeset in Times New Roman by Chic Graphics

Printed and bound in England by
CPI Group (UK) Ltd., Croydon, CR0 4YY

Pen & Sword Books Ltd incorporates the imprints of
Pen & Sword Archaeology, Atlas, Aviation, Battleground, Discovery,
Family History, History, Maritime, Military, Naval, Politics,
Railways, Select, Social History, Transport, True Crime, and
Claymore Press, Frontline Books, Leo Cooper, Praetorian Press,
Remember When, Seaforth Publishing and Wharncliffe.

For a complete list of Pen & Sword titles please contact
PEN & SWORD BOOKS LIMITED
47 Church Street, Barnsley, South Yorkshire, S70 2AS, England
E-mail: enquiries@pen-and-sword.co.uk
Website: www.pen-and-sword.co.uk

CONTENTS

Acknowledgements

The retreat from Mons has always held a fascination for me since I discovered that a family member - a lieutenant with 17/Field Company – fought at Mons and took part in the long trek south. Sadly, his diary account of the retreat was lost in September 1914 but Gerald survived, going on to win the DSO and bar and rising to the rank of brigadier general and, ultimately, the command of 93 Infantry Brigade. No mean feat for a sapper!

As always the writing of a book of this nature requires the help and support of a great many individuals and first and foremost I owe a great debt of gratitude to the men of the BEF who recorded their thoughts and experiences at the time, leaving a wonderful legacy for future generations of historians to read. Many of these accounts are held by the Imperial War Museum and to the staff in the reading room I extend my thanks for their kindness and patience. Members of staff at the National Archives at Kew have also provided much valued help and assistance, as have those at the Leeds University Archive and the Grenadier Guards' archive at Princess Gate.

It would also have been difficult to write an account of the retreat without following in the footsteps of the men who took part and in doing that I must thank those who have accompanied me on numerous visits to the retreat battlefields, in particular Dave Rowland, Tom Waterer, Paul Webster, Bill Dobbs, Jon Cooksey and Sebastian Lauden. Sebastian has been of particular help in translating German regimental histories and ensuring that, where possible, the German side of the encounters I have described have been taken into account.

I thank Pen and Sword Books for permission to quote from *Fifteen Rounds a Minute* and Tom Donovan Publishing for permission to reproduce the map of the retreat from *Dishonoured.* In the search for photographic material I have been unable – despite repeated attempts – to trace all the copyright holders, I must crave the indulgence of literary executors or copyright holders where these efforts have so far failed and would urge them to contact me through the publisher to enable me to give due acknowledgement at the first opportunity.

Finally – but by no means least – I must extend my gratitude to my wife Joan, who has yet again been abandoned in the wake of trips across the water and forsaken by the keyboard as looming manuscript deadlines prompt absences from family life and the washing-up!

Jerry Murland
Coventry
January 2014

Series Editor's Introduction

With books in the Battleground Europe series on Mons, Le Cateau, Néry and the Aisne, one of the biggest gaps that remained was the story of I Corps' retreat from Mons, given the fairly straight-forward participation of the BEF in the counter stroke on the Marne. With three books on the fighting around Ypres and Messines in the autumn of 1914 all being published by the autumn of this year, the major action remaining to be covered lies along the Lys, in which I, III and latterly the Indian Army Corps battled it out with the Germans in the October.

In recent months I have been fortunate to be able to revisit the battlefields of I Corps after a long absence – indeed it is some twenty five years since I ventured so far south. This time I was armed with Jerry Murland's *Retreat and Rearguard*, an excellent and well illustrated account of the events of that summer and autumn a hundred years ago from the perspective of the BEF.

I have also been working on the trilogy of books on Ypres 1914, with Jack Sheldon providing the story as seen from the German perspective. This period of time spent on the 1914 Expeditionary Force has been a fascinating one, combining with the work done on Le Cateau almost a decade ago and Mons almost twenty years ago, when revising for print the Battleground on Mons, the work of that great enthusiast of the First World War – and especially of his beloved 42nd (East Lancs) Division – the late Jack Horsfall.

A few things have struck me as a consequence of all of this work on the BEF in 1914, reinforced by what Jerry has written here about I Corps.

The first is that I have increased my admiration for the achievement of the BEF in 1914.

Many people write of the destruction of the old regular army in 1914, which is true: but only to a point. It is a fact that a very significant part of the regular officer corps were killed or permanently disabled in the fighting of 1914. Nowhere else was this to have more long term significance than in the loss of a disproportionately high number of staff qualified officers; the impact of this was to be felt for months to come. It is also true that the loss of skilled NCOs was almost as significant in the slow building up of the fighting capability of the massively expanded army that Britain was soon to field in France. But, interestingly, it was not so much the regular army that was destroyed but rather its pool of reservists and, rather less significantly, special reservists. Overall, at least 60% of the army that embarked for France in August 1914 came from these sources. Admittedly, three more regular divisions – the 4th, the 6th and the 7th and more cavalry formations – were with the BEF by the time the fighting at Ypres came to an end, with the 8th Division arriving just as matters had passed the crucial point. But even these formations, though generally with far fewer reservists, still had a significant element of them in their ranks.

The second point lay in the generally fair to good performance of all levels of command with the notable exception of the British GHQ under Sir John French. He (not helped by his dysfunctional staff) seems to have been out of his depth in coalition warfare; though it has to be noted that this was far from being exclusively a result of his own shortcomings. Lanrezac, the commander of the neighbouring French Fifth Army, should take the bulk of the blame for the disastrous mistrust that built up between him and the BEF. Otherwise the BEF conducted itself pretty well, allowing for poor communications which led to unnecessary casualties and losses, be it at Audregnies or at Le Cateau, at Le Grand Fayt or Étreux. The flexibility of the BEF was, without a doubt, best shown at Ypres, when command was often dislocated by the casualties amongst senior officers, from divisional commander down to company commanders, and the ability of those junior to step into the breach and to maintain a robust and, in the end, successful, defence. There were unforced errors and wrong decisions were undoubtedly made, but the general impression that I have is of a force that fought well and effectively, even if not with an overall significance on the war that British 'myth' tends to give it.

The third area is one of admiration for the endurance of the men of the BEF, many of whom had been in civilian occupations only very recently – in a great many cases not much more than a fortnight before action commenced. We tend to look at maps and see locations that are relatively close to each other and not take into account what it was like to be doing all this interminable marching, especially as much of it was conducted either under fire or under the threat of it. Add to this the need to be almost permanently alert for an attack, grabbing a few hours' rest more often than not in the open or in inadequate accommodation and receiving limited and decidedly unexciting rations for the most part. The distance covered on poor roads was considerable (spare a thought for the Germans as well); they were either mud or chalk tracks or pavéd roads, the latter having a frequently horrendous impact on men's feet – the majority of whom were wearing new boots. Movement, in any case, was not simply a matter of walking along clear highways – the roads were thronging with refugees and with units and even formations of the French army either trying to use the same road or moving across the British line of retreat. I think few people appreciate just how much space on a road just a brigade of infantry needed – some three miles, allowing for all the elements that were in support of its four infantry battalions.

The fourth point lies in the tendency of the national consciousness to neglect the contribution of the allies: the Belgians had their heroic days at Ypres in October and November 1914; the contribution of the Russians made von Motke take the fateful decision to withdraw three army corps from his right flank at a crucial time and, ironically, they were to make no difference to the events in the east; the French bore the brunt of the fighting. Joffre made numerous mistakes, but he was the mastermind of the Marne and remained calm under tremendous pressure. The reality was that the BEF was significant – sometimes because it actually existed rather than what it achieved – but not crucial for most of the 1914 campaign. True, Joffre would have had to rethink his Marne attack if there had been no BEF in position at the time; true, also, that the BEF enabled the French to extend their line at Mons, which was also very important. But the really big battles of the late summer and the early autumn of 1914 were fought elsewhere. It was at Ypres that the BEF played a very significant role – but even then we tend to forget just how many troops the French army committed to that ferocious battle.

This book takes you to parts of France well off the usual battle field tour route – indeed, some of it in parts of France that were to see nothing or hardly anything of the BEF again during the war. Time spent touring here is well worthwhile, amongst others: Landrecies and Maroilles (the latter better known to the British now for its cheese than for anything that happened in 1914); the sleepy village of Le Grand Fayt, with what I think is a unique burial arrangement of casualties from both sides in its communal cemetery; the heroic and sad stand of the Munsters at Étreux, so tellingly illustrated by the beautiful resting place of the men who were killed there; the largely unspoilt battlefield at Cerizy (even allowing for a motorway on its eastern edge); and the haunting Guards Grave Cemetery at Villers Cotterêts, set in the brooding atmosphere of a great forest.

A tour of I Corps' route brings new insights and understanding to a part of the campaign that is, admittedly, often well described in numerous books on the Retreat, in parts of regimental histories or in first rate memoirs. However, seeing the ground is all but essential in the search for an adequate understanding of what happened in those long, hot (although occasionally stormy) days of the summer of 1914.

Nigel Cave
Caudry, June 2014.

Introduction

This book departs from the usual Battleground Europe format in that it covers part of an enormous battlefield of some 200 miles in length and as such does not centre on a specific location. Battlefield visitors intending to make the historic journey that British troops undertook in August and September 1914 will find this volume a suitable companion to two guidebooks published by Pen and Sword Books that cover the BEF retreat in great detail and offer a number of local walks and bike rides exploring specific rearguard actions fought by both I and II Corps. *The Retreat from Mons 1914: North* covers the ground from Mons to Le Cateau, while *The Retreat from Mons 1914: South* takes in the fighting from Étreux to points south of the Marne.

As the title suggests, this book is focused almost entirely on the route taken by Lieutenant General Sir Douglas Haig and the two infantry divisions of I Corps, a focus that has been dictated by the course of events which unfolded on 24 August after Sir John French - who had been appointed Commander-in-Chief on 30 July - and General Headquarters (GHQ) were confronted by the Forêt de Mormal, which lay in the path of the retreat. The principle II Corps engagements at Mons, Le Cateau and Néry have been well documented in the three Battleground Europe titles of the same name. Unfortunately the space available in this book means that it is impossible to relate the experiences of every unit of I Corps that took part in the retreat but what I hope I have done is provide enough of the story to enable you to gain an understanding of what took place and why, thereby providing a catalyst for further reading and research.

The retreat began less than three weeks after the declaration of war and a mere three days after the BEF had assembled at Maubeuge - a rude awakening for British forces and a sharp introduction to European warfare! There were no trenches at this point in the war and as the intention was to advance north from Mons, few detailed maps of the ground south of Le Cateau were available apart from those hastily scrambled together or those that were 'liberated' en route. Indeed there are numerous tales of battalions navigating their way south using cycling maps and even French railway maps.

Students of the retreat will be well aware that the two corps of the British Expeditionary Force (BEF) followed different routes to the Marne after GHQ decided that the Forêt de Mormal should be avoided by passing either side of it. From that point on Sir Douglas Haig and General Sir Horace Smith-Dorrien were destined to follow parallel paths meeting again only after 1 September – over a week later. Those parallel paths, which continued after 25 August, were brought about largely by the I Corps encounter with units of the German *7th Division* at Landrecies, an encounter that was behind Haig's decision to march south from Maroilles and by-pass Le Cateau.

In order to make the book more accessible I have divided Haig's retreat into three stages, each of which is supported by a tour that takes the battlefield visitor to the battlegrounds described in the text. Opportunity has also been provided for those who wish to get out of their vehicle and walk some of the ground that was fought over almost a century ago. Where you are able to I would highly recommend you do so, as it is only by walking the ground that you can get a full appreciation of what took place and why.

As the BEF withdrew from Mons on 23 August 1914, the role of cavalry regiments and their supporting Royal Horse Artillery (RHA) batteries proved to be of vital importance in providing an essential screen between the pursuing enemy and the infantry rearguard. Major John Darling, who served in the 20th Hussars as a captain during the retreat, was aware that many felt the cavalry had a much easier time than the infantry in the 200 mile long retirement from Mons. 'Constantly we find a German attack was developing just as the time had come for us to retire', he wrote, 'or that we retired just as an attack was developing'. But this was 'the very essence of a rearguard action – to make the enemy deploy, thus wasting his time, then, when he had made his maximum deployment, to slip away, thus causing him further delay in reforming column of route'. To this end I have included the rearguard action at Cerizy, which was fought by 5 Cavalry Brigade. Brigadier General Chetwode's cavalry brigade, along with J Battery RHA, was attached to I Corps at the time of the retreat and spent much of their time acting as flank guard. It was while they were on the western bank of the Oise that they encountered the German Guard Cavalry Division at Cerizy.

British accounts of the retreat tend to gloss over the fact that in the great scheme of things the BEF was very much a minor player over an ever extending battleground that saw six French and seven German Armies in the field; but the British soldier on the ground would have been only too well aware of his French allies being alongside him and in some cases even competing for the same stretch of road along which he was retiring.

So what was it about this 'contemptible little army' that enabled it to survive one of the longest retreats in its history? The British *Official History* claimed that the BEF was incomparably well trained, well organized and equipped. Well trained it might have been, but when it came to fighting in a major European conflict there were still some harsh lessons which had to be learned. One of these was the value of good staff work and its impact upon effective command and control. It became clear as the retreat unfolded that the lack of experience of senior officers in handling large bodies of troops on the battlefield certainly contributed to errors of judgement on occasion. At battalion and brigade level the decisions made by Lieutenant Colonel Abercrombie in the deployment of his Connaught Rangers at Grand Fayt has to be questioned as does Brigadier General Ivor Maxse's handling of the Étreux episode, in which the men of the 2nd Battalion Royal Munster Fusiliers (2/RMF) were forced to fight a desperate rearguard action.

A high proportion of the men who went to war with the BEF were reservists, former soldiers who had served their period of active engagement and had an obligation to return to the colours in time of national emergency. These were supplemented by men of the Special Reserve. The Special Reservists were similar in many ways to the part-time territorial soldiers in that they were essentially civilians who undertook regular periods of military training but, unlike the men of the Territorial Force, they were liable for overseas service. The actual number of reservists who went to war in August 1914 is quite staggering; it is estimated that 60 per cent of the BEF's manpower came from its reservists and it was these men who suffered the most, due to problems arising from their lack of military fitness and the newness of their boots on the long marches from Mons.

Many units had, in fact, already been on the road for two or three days before arriving at Mons on 22 August; in some cases marching up to forty miles or more from railheads such as that at Landrecies. For many of those men it was forty miles too far in new boots and was a problem that would intensify over the course of the retreat as punishing daily marches (see Appendix I) in the heat of an August sun took their toll of men who were unable to keep pace with their units. Although march discipline in many units kept the men together, some days were 'so hot that the men were falling out and even dropping down in the road in dozens'. The more fortunate were collected up in carts and wagons but many of the stragglers were invariably left behind to await their inevitable capture. Nevertheless, every rearguard action fought – whether a major action or a passing skirmish - was instrumental in creating and maintaining the vital gap between the

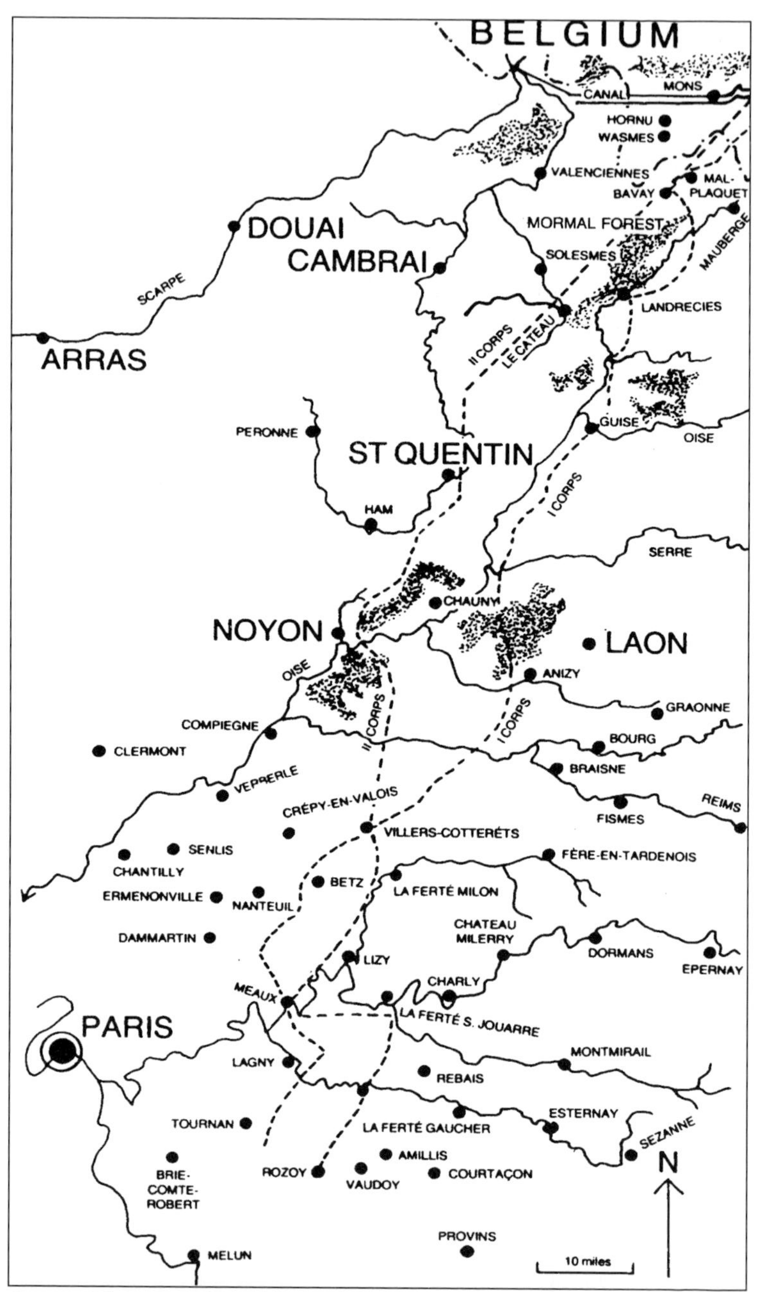

A map of the retreat from Mons originally published in *Dishonoured* showing the approximate routes followed by I and II Corps during the retreat. The two separate paths taken by Douglas Haig and Horace Smith-Dorrien are seen only meeting twice: at Villers Cotterêts and Meaux. Compare this map with that taken from the Official History which shows the path taken by units of III Corps.

pursuing German forces and a very tired, and often extremely hungry, BEF.

In the view of the author the retreat cannot be considered a victory as has sometimes been suggested, GHQ lost control of the retreating BEF soon after 24 August and would not regain any semblance of command until 5 September. The BEF escaped envelopment at Mons by the skin of its teeth and it was only the regimental officers who – along with their senior NCOs – held the battalions together on the retreat itself and ensured that the BEF was largely intact when it came to the Battles of the Marne and the Aisne. If the term victory is to be used at all it should be applied to the officers and men of the BEF and the regimental system that distinguished them.

The Retreat from Mons

German military forces crossed the border into Belgium at two minutes past eight on the morning of 4 August 1914 and were met by a fusillade of shots as Belgian gendarmes opened fire near the frontier town of Gemmerich. This blatant disregard for Belgian neutrality by Germany opened a conflict that was to last for over four years, cut great swathes though the quiet countryside of Belgium and Northern France and left behind a trail of cemeteries and memorials to mark the war that was supposed to end all wars.

German forces in the west numbered some 1,500,000 men, who were deployed in seven army groups along the Belgian and French borders, with the *First Army* on the extreme right opposite Liège and the *Seventh Army* holding the left flank in Alsace. Their invasion strategy for France and Belgium – first formulated by Count Alfred von Schlieffen in 1905 – had been planned to the last detail, taking into account what they hoped would be every unforeseen event that might impact on the timetable of attack and advance. Schlieffen's plan was for a war on two fronts: a swift and decisive incursion into France which would be concluded before Russian forces in the east would be able to mobilize effectively. Staff officers at German General Headquarters (OHL) were confident that their calculations of Russian railway mileage and the limitations this would impose on Russian Army mobilization would allow their armies in the west to overwhelm France and then move enough divisions to the east to defeat Russia.

German infantry from the First Army on the march towards Mons.

The German deployment

Thus in August 1914, as the countdown to war began, the German *Sixth* and *Seventh Armies* were in position along the Alsace and Lorraine front, the *Fourth* and *Fifth Armies* were poised to invade France through the Ardennes and Luxembourg and, on the right wing, the *First, Second* and *Third Armies* were ready to advance through neutral Belgium. The three armies of the German right wing were commanded by relatively old men, two of whom, General Alexander von Kluck, commanding the *First Army* and General Klaus von Bülow of the *Second Army*, were veterans of the Franco-Prussian War of 1870. Although both commanders were 68 years old, the more energetic and aggressive command style of von Kluck often clashed with that of the more cautious von Bülow.

The German First Army was commanded by Alexander von Kluck.

Klaus von Bülow, the commander of the German Second Army.

Von Kluck's *First Army* was deployed on the extreme right wing of the German armies in the west. His orders were to attack the left flank of the French Army and drive them back, ultimately enveloping Paris before turning east to trap the French between the Franco-German border and the German Armies advancing from Alsace and Lorraine, thereby bringing a rapid conclusion to the war. Although the *First Army* had the greatest offensive striking power, a density of about 18,000 men per mile of front, they had the longest distance to march. It was von Kluck's men who would first encounter the BEF at Mons.

Britain Mobilizes for War

At 4.30pm on 4 August 1914, British land forces were ordered to mobilize for war against Germany in response to the violation of Belgian neutrality. Almost immediately nearly 60,000 reservists began to pour into regimental depots as the smooth machinery of mobilization organized Britain's army for its first war on the continental mainland of Europe in almost a hundred years. Screened by the ships of the Royal Navy, the embarkation of the BEF began on 11 August, with up to thirty-seven ships per day carrying men, equipment and supplies to Rouen, Le

Havre and Boulogne. After landing in France, troops were dispatched to nearby rest camps before embarking on lengthy train journeys to the BEF forward assembly area near Maubeuge. By 20 August assembly was complete; it had all gone like clockwork.

In command of the BEF was Sir John French who, at 61 years old, had made his reputation commanding the British Cavalry Division in the South African War. His command of the celebrated cavalry charge at Klip Drift and the subsequent relief of Kimberley propelled his face and name onto the front pages of the British press and at the end of the war he was one of only a handful of senior officers to emerge with their reputations intact. Nevertheless, this brave and resourceful soldier, who was more at home leading troops in the field, lacked the basic mastery of the management of strategic command. He was one of the few senior officers in the BEF who had not attended the Staff College at Camberley.

Sir John French was appointed to command the BEF on 30 July 1914.

Compounded by fears in England of a German invasion of the home country and the recent trouble in Ireland over Home Rule, the British Government was initially cautious, committing only four of its six intended infantry divisions and one cavalry division to the BEF. Thus, the fighting strength of the British force which went to war was made up of I Corps (1st and 2nd Divisions) commanded by Lieutenant General Sir Douglas Haig, II Corps (3rd and 5th Divisions) commanded by Lieutenant General Sir James Grierson and a Cavalry Division under the command of Major General Edmund Allenby. In addition there were the five infantry battalions of 19 Brigade designated for the protection and maintenance of the lines of communication. Sadly, Grierson died from a heart attack on the way to Le Cateau on 17 August and was replaced by General Sir Horace Smith-Dorrien two days later.

Lieutenant General Sir Douglas Haig, commander of I Corps in 1914.

Edmund 'Bull' Allenby commanded the Cavalry Division during the retreat from Mons.

Unquestionably Haig saw himself as the more suitable choice for the top job and after the demise of Grierson must have viewed the arrival of a more senior colleague in the form of Smith-Dorrien as a setback to his ambitions. Haig apparently felt no personal hostility towards Smith-Dorrien but there were several occasions when it appeared he may have deliberately avoided supporting his II Corps colleague.

General Sir Horace Smith-Dorrien replaced James Grierson as commander of II Corps after Grierson's untimely death.

The BEF and French Deployment

The BEF's assembly area was a narrow strip running from Maubeuge in the north east to Le Cateau in the south west, where Sir John French had established his GHQ in a school house in the centre of the town. On its right was XVIII Corps of the French Fifth Army and on its immediate left the French 84th Territorial Division. The French Plan XVII, as it became known, was outlined to Sir John at French Supreme Headquarters (GQG) by the French Commander-in-Chief, General Joseph Joffre. In concept it was quite simple: the Third and Fourth French Armies were to strike northeast through the Ardennes against the rear of the German Army advancing through Belgium, while the French Fifth Army of General Charles Lanrezac, together with the BEF, would advance into Belgium north of the River Meuse and outflank the right wing of the German Army in a pincer movement.

Charles Lanrezac, commander of the French Fifth Army.

Unfortunately the optimism expressed by the French Commander-in-Chief was not shared by the commander of the Fifth Army, General Charles Lanrezac, who was becoming increasingly concerned – and quite rightly as it turned out – by reports of the true strength of the advancing German forces, a factor apparently being ignored by Joffre at GQG in spite of intelligence to the contrary.

The British advance into Belgium was a short one; the German *First* and *Second Armies* were rapidly closing from the north and, to make matters worse, the German *Third Army,* under General Max von Hausen, was moving swiftly towards them from the east. Lanrezac's reluctance to advance in accordance with the wishes of GQG almost certainly

Max von Hausen and his Third Army clashed with Lanrezac during the Battle of Charleroi on 22 August.

saved the Fifth Army and the BEF from destruction. However, none of this was apparent early on 22 August as the BEF moved into their positions at Mons to align with Lanrezac's Fifth Army, then assembled along the line of the River Sambre between Namur and Charleroi.

Regular and effective liaison between army commanders is vital if they are to co-operate with one another and share intelligence. Unfortunately the relationship between Sir John French and Charles Lanrezac got off to a disastrous start and never really recovered thereafter. From the moment of their first meeting on 17 August at Rethel both men took an instant dislike to each other. Lanrezac's obvious sarcasm and distrust of his British allies was not lost on those who were present at the meeting and, as Lieutenant Edward Spears – acting as a liaison officer between the BEF and the French Fifth Army – later observed, Lanrezac's indifference to the BEF and complete disregard for any form of co-operation had a profound impact on the opening phase of the campaign; the consequences of which resulted in a running sore of distrust that remained a permanent obstacle between Sir John and his Fifth Army counterpart. Thus, with GQG still minimising intelligence reports regarding the strength of the German right wing and communication with the Fifth Army almost non-existent, the BEF was very much thrown back on its own ability to gather intelligence.

Lieutenant Edward Spears served as the British liaison officer to the French Fifth Army.

Unfortunately that intelligence was largely disregarded by GHQ. On 21 August George Barrow rode into Mons and took over the railway telephone office. For the next twelve hours he contacted all 'the possible and impossible places in Belgium not known yet to be in German hands'. From the replies received he was able to get a fairly accurate picture of the German advance, a picture that indicated the German right wing was much further west than had at first been realized. GHQ chose to ignore this new intelligence, suggesting that it was exaggerated, adding the instruction that the Cavalry Division was not to become seriously engaged.

First contact with the enemy

It was not long before British cavalry patrols reported their first clashes with the forward units of the German *9th Cavalry Division* and this, together with reconnaissance provided by the RFC, began to reveal the advance of the German *IX* (General von Quast) and *III Army Corps* (General von Lochow) and the presence of the German *II Army Corps* under General von Linsigen, marching south west along a route that would bring it outside the British left flank at Mons.

Captain Lionel Charleton (above) and Second Lieutenant Vivian Wadham landed their Bleriot XI-2 amongst German infantry on 22 August.

The RFC reconnaissance flights had been filing reports on German troop movements since 19 August. On Saturday 22 August, twelve reconnaissance flights revealed the presence of large bodies of troops moving in the direction of Mons and several aircraft reported coming under fire. But it was the flight undertaken by Captain Lionel Charlton and Second Lieutenant Vivian Wadham which finally confirmed the scale of the approaching storm. Having landed near Grammont in their Bleriot XI-2, it did not take the British airmen long to discover that:

> *We had landed absolutely in the middle of a large concentration of German troops, the nearest of which was about a quarter of an hour's walk away. After collecting some quite good information ... we hurriedly switched on the engine and started off hoping for the best. When about 500 feet up, we flew plumb over a German brigade halted for the dinner hour ... I imagine someone must have said: 'By Jove! There goes an English aeroplane: let's have it.' At any rate every man jack jumped to his feet and loosed off at us.*

On landing, the aircraft was found to have over forty bullet holes in addition to a badly damaged spar. They had been very fortunate. Charlton himself had a very near miss; as he clambered out of the machine he

The Bleriot XI-2 of the type flown by Charleton and Wadham.

found his safety belt had been shot through by a German bullet. Incredibly, Sir John's reaction to this intelligence was lukewarm and it was not until he had confirmation – in the form of a very concerned Lieutenant Spears – that he began to place any faith in it.

The predicament that faced the commander-in-chief on 22 August hinged on GHQ's understanding that both the BEF and the French Fifth Army were to advance at the earliest possible moment. With the BEF moving up to positions along the Mons-Condé Canal, Sir John was on his way to discuss the joint offensive with Lanrezac when he met Spears on the roadside. The young lieutenant had actually been on his way to see Sir John and took the opportunity to relay his fears that Lanrezac was seriously considering remaining on the south bank of the Sambre and not advancing as had been intended. He also shared with his commander-in-chief the view from the Fifth Army Intelligence Bureau that the far-flung German movements to the west could only mean an enveloping movement on a huge scale. More importantly, he confirmed the presence of the *II Army Corps,* which had been identified by the RFC reconnaissance flights.

The pincer movement envisaged by Joffre and Plan XVII was now taking place in reverse and the BEF was in danger of being attacked on two sides. The fact that this information was relayed to the BEF via Spears and not through official channels gives some indication of the extent of the ill-feeling extant between Sir John and Charles Lanrezac. Consequently, Sir John French's planned meeting with Lanrezac on 22 August 1914 never took place. On hearing from Spears that the Fifth Army commander was at Mettet, Sir John judged it too far to travel and, despite Spears almost pleading with French to change his mind, Sir John returned to Le Cateau.

On the evening of 22 August any shred of optimism that might have prevailed was dashed when the French Fifth Army was alerted to the presence of the *XII Saxon Corps* at Dinant, threatening the Fifth Army's right flank. General Lanrezac concluded that his only course of action was to fall back to a new position and he thus informed Joffre. To his shame he did not see fit to share his decision with Sir John French, who was still under the impression that all was well on his right flank. Once again it was the resolute Spears who brought the bad news to GHQ, finally prompting Sir John to cancel the planned advance of the BEF. There was a further rather bizarre episode that night when an officer from Lanrezac's staff arrived at Le Cateau with a request for the BEF to attack the right flank of the German *Second Army*. It was an impossible demand and the British reply was cordial and to the effect that they would hold their current positions at Mons for twenty four hours.

While GHQ was apparently unaware until a few hours before of the actual strength of the German forces confronting them, von Kluck was just as surprised to find both corps of the BEF at Mons. On the morning of 22 August the German *First Army* was still under the impression that the BEF would appear in the Lille area and had landed six divisions at Boulogne and Calais. Even though German *First Army* intelligence had reported British troops in the Mons area and British aircraft had been observed over Louvain as early as 20 August, *First Army* orders for 23 August anticipated an easy day's march south, expecting to meet the BEF either at Lille or Maubeuge.

It was only on the morning of 22 August that the German *9th Cavalry Division* encountered elements of 4/Dragoon Guards on their way to Ath and reported it. So intent was he on continuing his wide sweeping movement to the west that von Kluck chose to ignore the possibility that the skirmish with British cavalry and the presence of RFC reconnaissance aircraft was an indication that the BEF lay in his path.

23 August – The Battle of Mons

On the morning of 23 August 1914 the BEF was in position thus: Smith-Dorrien's II Corps lined the canal between Mons and Condé facing north, while Douglas Haig's I Corps was posted along the Beaumont–Mons road facing northeast. To the west the cavalry guarded the canal crossings as far as Condé. It was a battleground that would see only Smith-Dorrien's II Corps engaged with the German *First Army* along the canal, which in itself had a serious weakness at its eastern point where it formed

The Grand Place at Mons in 1914, taken after German occupation.

British troops begin their long retreat to the Marne.

a salient around Nimy. It was a weakness that worried Smith-Dorrien to such an extent that he had prepared a more defensible line a few miles further back along a line that ran through Dour – Frameries – Paturages. But the drama was building quickly and events to the east now dictated the next moves of the BEF. At 8.00pm on 23 August, GHQ at Le Cateau finally received word from Joffre that French intelligence had underestimated the strength of German forces opposing the BEF, information that was already only too apparent to Smith-Dorrien's II Corps, which, by now, was retiring to its second position south of Mons. Yet even in possession of this conclusive evidence, Sir John stubbornly clung to his belief that advance was still a possibility. His message to II Corps timed at 8.40pm that evening ordered them to stand firm and strengthen their new positions during the night. By the time the British II Corps received this signal General Lanrezac had already ordered the general retirement of his Fifth Army and once again had not seen fit to inform the British. It was left to Spears to make the journey to Le Cateau to inform Sir John, who, with no alternative left open to him, finally decided at midnight to retire. The retreat had begun.

Stage 1

Mons to Le Grand Fayt

This section covers the move south from Mons and the decision by GHQ to divide the BEF on either side of the Forêt de Mormal. This is the point at which Douglas Haig and I Corps became separated from Smith-Dorrien's II Corps and continued their retreat east of the route taken by II Corps. From this juncture the two corps commanders fought their own retreat and were only destined to converge briefly on 1 September. We also look at the pivotal rearguard action at Landrecies, which was fought on 25 August, and the two smaller engagements at Maroilles and Le Grand Fayt.

Background

Sir John's decision to order the retreat late on 23 August took little account of the logistics of movement. That aside, the manner in which he chose to inform his corps commanders of his decision was in many ways responsible for the very costly rearguard actions that Smith-Dorrien's two divisions and the Cavalry Corps had to fight over the course of 24 August. His decision came some fifteen hours after the historic meeting at the Château de la Roche at Sars-la Bruyère. General Smith-Dorrien based himself and his staff here prior to the Battle of Mons

The Château de la Roche at Sars-la Bruyère, the venue for the meeting of senior BEF commanders on 23 August. The meeting took place in a downstairs room to the left of the steps.

but the château is more renowned for the meeting that took place here at 5.30am on 23 August between Sir John French and his three principal field commanders. Also present at the meeting – which began an hour or so before the first shots were fired at Obourg – was Major General Sir William Robertson, the Quarter-Master General and Major General Sir Archibald Murray, the BEF Chief of Staff. In the château itself this meeting has been commemorated with a plaque fixed to the wall just outside the downstairs room in which the meeting was convened. What actually took place at this conference is difficult to piece together as both Smith-Dorrien and Sir John differ in their accounts, accounts which were altered in their subsequent memoirs. Colin Ballard – who commanded the infantry at the Battle of Audregnies on 24 August – wrote after the war in his biography of Smith-Dorrien that retreat was not discussed at the meeting. That said, it is difficult to believe it was not on the agenda, particularly as Sir John French left Sir Archibald Murray at the château 'to give orders for such a movement should it become necessary'. However, whatever the truth may be, we can be sure that the situation facing the BEF was discussed at length and it is highly likely that Sir John did indeed order his corps commanders to be ready to move. Whether this movement was in retreat or advance is unclear. What is clear is that Sir John French had still not fully accepted the desperate nature of the situation the BEF was in and as late as 7.15pm on 23 August, after II Corps had withdrawn from the Condé Canal to their overnight positions, Smith-Dorrien asked permission to fall back on Bavay if necessary, a request that was refused. Yet only four hours later the order to retire on Bavay eventually came from Sir John French, who had by that time arrived back at his Le Cateau GHQ.

Sir Archibald Murray, Chief of Staff to Sir John French.

Part of the problem lay with the poor quality of advice he was receiving from his sub Chief of Staff, Henry Wilson and the French GQG and part lay with his remoteness from the battlefield. From Le Cateau, GHQ was in

Major General Henry Wilson was accused of giving poor advice to Sir John French.

direct contact with I Corps, but there was no such link with Smith-Dorrien and II Corps or with Allenby's Cavalry HQ at Élouges. Consequently, when the three Chiefs of Staff were summoned to Le Cateau to be informed of the decision to retire, Brigadier General Johnnie Gough was able to wire the orders almost immediately through to I Corps informing Haig of the change of plan.

At 9.00pm on the evening of 23 August Edward Spears was summoned to GHQ by Sir John French's Chief of Staff, Archie Murray. Spears was told that the BEF would continue its retreat the next day as the threat to its left was still apparent and as Lanrezac's Fifth Army was a day's march to the rear of the British right, the BEF had no choice but to keep pace. Spears dutifully relayed the message to Lanrezac's HQ at Aubenton at 10.00pm only to receive the news that the whole of the French Fifth Army was to retire south of Le Cateau the next morning to a new line: La Capelle-Hirson-Mezières.

The I Corps dispositions at dawn on 24 August

At dawn the BEF were holding their positions south of Mons, roughly seventeen miles long. The 1st Division were facing northeast along a line running from Grand Reng through Rouveroy to Givry, while the 2nd Division – facing north – were on a line running from Harmignies to Bougnies. With new instructions issued from the I Corps HQ near Bonnet at 2.00am, the 1st Division began their retirement at 4.00am followed at 4.45am by the 2nd Division, with 4 (Guards) Brigade, 5 Cavalry Brigade and two brigades of artillery detailed as rearguard under the command of Brigadier General Henry Horne. Despite some shelling and small enemy cavalry patrols, their movement was largely untroubled. It was, as Major Lord Bernard Gordon Lennox noted in his diary, the start of a 'long and tiring retirement, beginning at Mons and finishing up near Paris, and I don't think any of us wish to go through such a trying time again'.

Brigadier General Henry Horne commanded the I Corps rearguard on 24 August.

Major Gordon Lennox was a company commander with the 2nd Battalion Grenadier Guards (2/Grenadiers) and his diary, written up on the march south, provides us with a good account of the retreat from the perspective of a regimental officer. As 4 Guards Brigade retired they were pursued by 'ineffectual' shellfire, which Gordon Lennox could 'see bursting just ahead of us', but shellfire, it appears, was the least of their worries. What concerned them more was what was happening on the wider strategic front. 'Owing to the absolute secrecy which pervaded everything', wrote Gordon Lennox in his diary, 'no one knew what was going on anywhere: no one knows what one is driving at, where anyone is, what we have got against us, or anything at all, and what is told us generally turns out to be entirely wrong.' That night the battalion dug in at Quévy-le-Grand.

Major Bernard Gordon Lennox commanded Number 2 Company of the 2nd Battalion Grenadier Guards.

The Forêt de Mormal

Operational Order No 7, that gave details of the retirement on Le Cateau, had given Murray and the staff at GHQ some anxiety as they debated the difficulties of passing the thirty-five square miles of the Forêt de Mormal that stood between Bavay and Le Cateau. Just why there had not been a preliminary reconnaissance to ascertain whether any of the roads that ran through the forest were practical for marching infantry and their transports is another indication as to the uncertainty that existed at GHQ on 24 August. There appears to have been plenty of time for this vital reconnaissance to have taken place and A Squadron, North Irish Horse, who were serving as GHQ attached cavalry, were the ideal troops to carry it out. Murray's report to Haig later on the 24th stating the roads through the forest were unsuitable was apparently based on evidence from maps and may have suggested to Haig that a proper reconnaissance had been carried out. Even so, he did not order any reconnaissance of his own and in so doing he, and GHQ, left a large question mark unanswered.

GHQ, in its decision to avoid the forest, effectively split the two corps of the BEF and although Sir John intended Le Cateau would be the point at which they would reassemble, it would be another eight days and ninety more miles of retreat before Haig and Smith-Dorrien were reunited. In the circumstances there was only one sensible plan. Consequently, GHQ determined that Haig's I Corps would retire east of the forest in two columns: The 1st Division to cross the Sambre River at Hautmont and thence to Dompierre and the 2nd Division to cross at Pont sur Sambre and Berlaimont, and to march via Leval and Landrecies to Le Cateau. On the opposite side of the forest, II Corps would use two main routes, the direct Roman road that ran through Englefontaine and the more westerly road through Solesmes, to the line Le Cateau –

The Sambre at Hautmont. The 1st Division crossed the Sambre here on their way to Dompierre.

Caudry – Haucourt. Archie Murray, writing after the war, was adamant that in issuing the retirement orders he emphasised to Douglas Haig the importance of maintaining contact with II Corps.

A late start by I Corps on the morning of 25 August was not helped by having to share the roads with retiring French forces and the inevitable trail of civilian refugees with their belongings piled high on carts of all descriptions. Major Bernard Gordon Lennox recorded in his

The 2nd Battalion Grenadier Guards marching in review past Buckingham Palace on their way to Southampton. The salute is being taken by King George V.

diary 'a long and very hot march with continual gunning going on in our rear' noting, 'they seem pushing devils these Germans'. The march was not made any easier by two French reserve divisions using the same route as I Corps and General Sordet's French Cavalry Corps moving across their path at right angles from Avesnes en route to Cambrai. Haig must have decided early on that he was going to halt before he reached Le Cateau. Thus having motored down from Bavay and with Le Cateau still seven miles away, he established his overnight HQ at the small town of Landrecies on the southern extremity of the Forêt de Mormal. During the late afternoon and early evening the two divisions of I Corps halted in and around the town and further east at Maroilles and Avesnes, the last troops arriving by 6.00pm

The Rearguard Action at Landrecies – 25 August 1914

Major Bernard Gordon Lennox and the Grenadiers marched into Landrecies at 3.30pm, curious to know why they had passed no outposts on their way into the town. Continuing over the railway and on towards the square in perfect march order, Major George 'Ma' Jeffreys, who was at the head of the battalion, recognised the lanky form of the Brigade Major, Gerry Ruthven:

Major George Darell Jeffreys, taken in 1920 when he was GOC London District.

> *Who was standing by a street corner and asked him, "What about the outposts?" He said there were to be no outposts, as we were covered by other bodies of troops, and by the great Forêt de Mormal, through which there were no roads that could be used by troops.*

Jeffreys was right to be troubled, it was an omission that would have grated uncomfortably with any professional soldier but after a long and weary route march his primary concern for the moment was his men. Fortunately for all concerned, when a false alarm was sounded at 4.00pm by 'a French cavalryman who rode into town in a wild state of excitement' claiming the Germans were close behind him, the Coldstream Guards established an outpost line on the Le Quesnoy road just north of the Faubourg Soyeres. Captain Robert Whitbread and his company of the

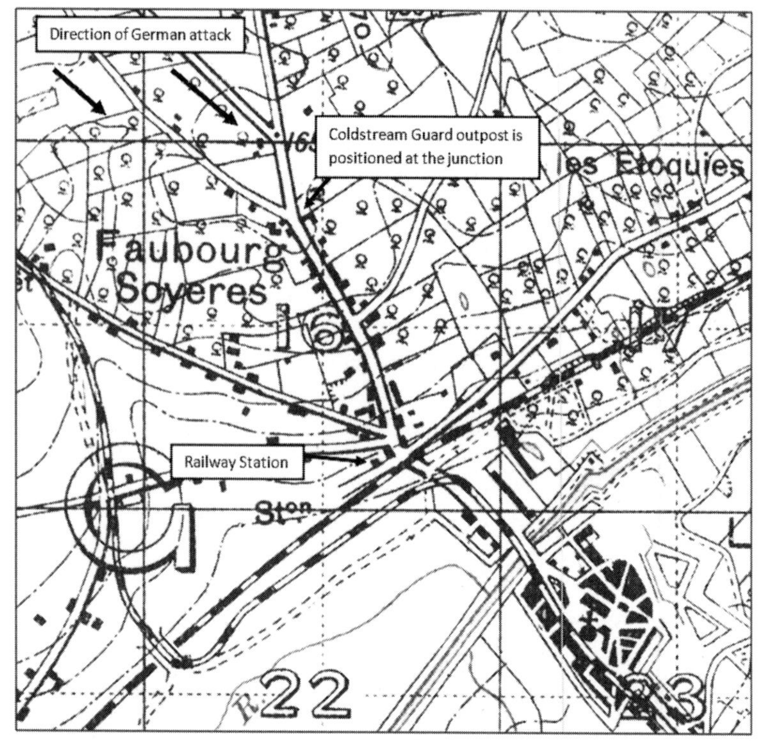

A contemporary 1914 map of Landrecies showing the location of the Coldstream Guards outpost north of Faubourg Soyeres in relation to the Sambre road bridge.

3rd Battalion Coldstream Guards had been in the town since 1.00pm and both officers and men were anticipating a good meal and a few hours undisturbed sleep, particularly as a dawn start had been ordered for the next morning:

> *About 4.00pm there was an alarm that the town was full of Germans, and we stood to arms for half an hour. About 7.45pm ... No 1 Company were ordered to fall in, and the officers of the company regretfully left an unfinished dinner to which they had just sat down. We marched out of the town across the railway, and met a cavalry patrol coming into the town, who told us there were no Germans within ten miles. We went about 600 yards past the station, here we met Monck* [Captain C H S Monck] *and some of his company (No 3) with the machine guns, under Bingham* [Lieutenant D C Bingham] *, in position across the main road at a point where two roads met in a V pointing toward the town.*

Dismissing the French cavalryman as a 'harmless lunatic', Bernard Gordon Lennox and the Grenadier officers of No 2 Company quickly settled into a comfortable billet and even found someone to cook their evening meal for them. It was to be a dinner that they too would leave unfinished:

> *We rushed out to hear heavy firing – musketry – going on just outside our end of the town. Everyone fell in hurriedly, there was a good deal of skurry but no disorder, when word came down that the Coldstream Guards outposts were being driven back.*

They had not quite been driven back but there was a moment or two when German troops nearly achieved their objective, Robert Whitbread was in conversation with Charlie Monck when the attack began:

> *We heard the noise of a large body of troops approaching, and also heard the noise of wheels. Then we thought we could hear German being talked when the leading men came to a strand of barbed wire which had been tied across the road 75 yards from the machine gun.*

Events now exploded into action as Monck gave the order to fire and the German infantrymen rushed forwards to seize the machine gun and bayonet the gunner, Private Thomas Robson. The Coldstream picquet ran forward, prompting the Germans to retire and leaving the battered machine gun behind them, but Robson's dying seconds on the trigger of the machine gun had wrought havoc amongst the enemy and the horses pulling the ammunition limbers and guns of *Field Artillery Regiment 4* (FAR 4) . The battery commander fell mortally wounded and the second in command was crushed beneath his horse. Pandemonium swept through the ranks before the authoritative voice of Colonel von Below, commanding *Infantry Regiment 27* (IR 27), ordered his men to extend on both sides of the road, an undertaking made more hazardous by the sustained volley fire from the Coldstream. The extent and ferocity of the attack left Whitbread and the Coldstream with little doubt that the attack was the vanguard of a much larger force:

> *We lay down in the road in readiness for a rush, we next heard some words of command in German and dimly saw a mass approaching, apparently slowly and without noise. When this mass was about fifty yards off we let them have five rounds rapid and a burst of machine gun fire...the same thing was repeated*

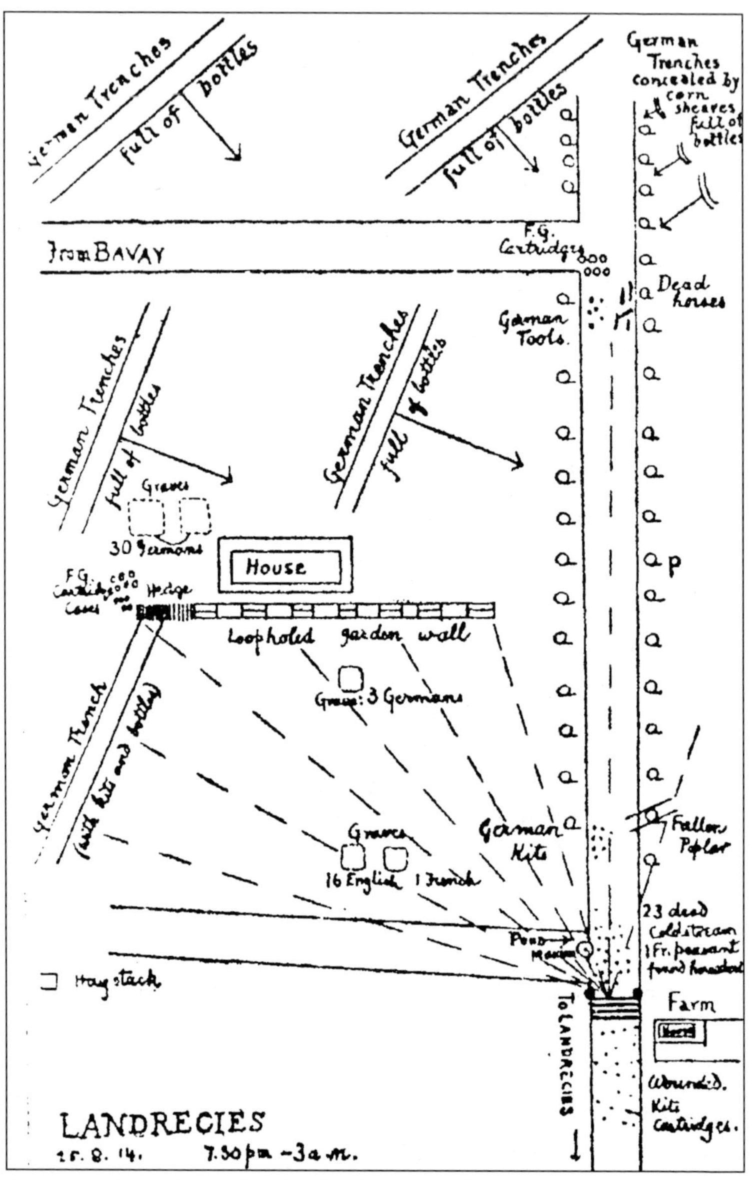

A map of the action at Landrecies drawn by Captain Hon Rupert Kepple, 3rd Battalion Coldstream Guards, after his capture.

several times, each rush being stopped by our fire. The din of rifles and machine gun fire drowned any sound of their advance and the flashes from rifles prevented us from seeing even dimly what had happened to the Germans.

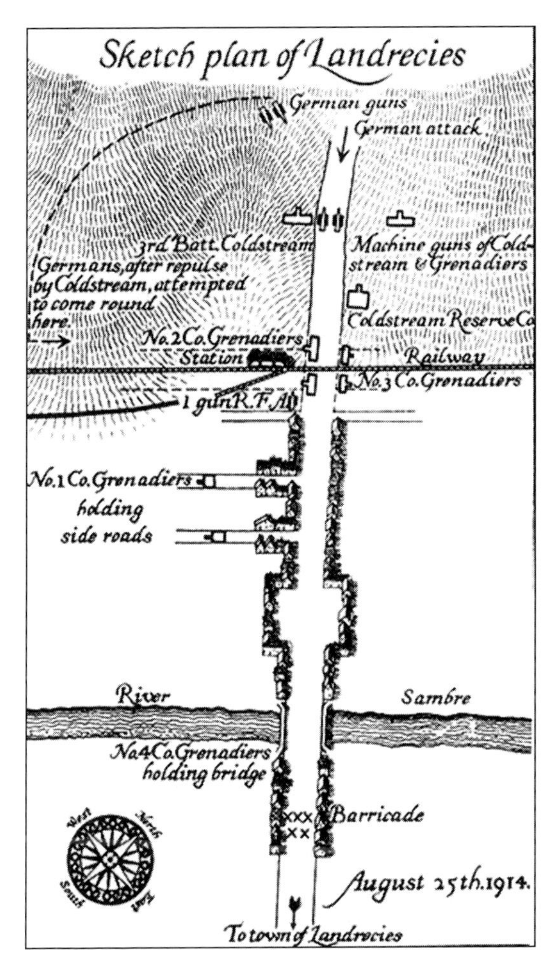

A rather simplified sketch plan of the Landrecies engagement originally drawn for *The Grenadier Guards in the Great War, Volume 1* on p. 30.

With the increasing noise of battle up ahead, the Grenadiers doubled up towards the firing line in the pouring rain to safeguard the other entrances to the town while the Irish Guards were employed putting the town in a state of defence. Gordon Lennox's company deployed on the right by the railway station, his men breaking into the empty houses to establish fields of fire down the streets that ran parallel to the station. Major Hamilton and No 1 Company held the side roads on the left, behind the station.

Charlie Monck's company had thwarted an attempt by units of *IR 27* to gain access to the town; they were probably as much surprised as the British at the encounter on the Le Quesnoy road and had fully expected to take the Sambre road bridge at the southern end of the town without

The Sambre road bridge Landrecies, probably taken after the Armistice.

opposition and find comfortable billets for the night. Now, thrown into confusion by the ferocity of the Coldstream defence, the commanding officer of *IR 27* sent his adjutant back for reinforcements, which arrived in the form of two companies from *Infantry Regiment 165* (IR 165).

In spite of the gathering mass of German infantry to their front, Whitbread and two companies of Coldstream – now under the command of Major Torquil Matheson – were managing to prevent any serious attack from developing until a field gun began firing at them over open sights:

> *We swept the hedges and surrounding ground with fire at intervals to stop them working their way under cover of the hedges to our flanks. Eventually the enemy worked up the road on our left and partially enfiladed the right half of our little line across the road, our line was moved back six yards but then, unluckily for us, the roof of a barn on our left was set on fire and our position on the road was lit up as if it were daylight. This enabled the enemy to bring up a gun on to the main road and they shelled our position at point blank range ... it was certainly very unpleasant to see their shells come all the way from the gun, the sparks accompanying each shell showed its passage in the darkness. Every time the enemy fired their gun they knocked out*

men all round me and I think they fired five shells when ....BIFF, I next remember finding myself tumbling about in a field with a wound in my head. I got out my field dressing but dropped it so held some wet grass to my head to stop the bleeding and called for help.

From the Grenadiers' positions at the railway station they could see the gun being fired by the light of the burning stack until it was knocked out by one of the two British guns that had been brought up in reply. But what they did not witness was 28 year old Lance Corporal George Wyatt run out under fire on two separate occasions and extinguish the blazing stack which was revealing the Coldstream's positions. It was a very brave act from an individual who had been walking the beat as a Barnsley policeman before he was called up on 5 August. His subsequent Victoria Cross was presented by the king at Buckingham Palace in March 1916.

Lance Corporal George Wyatt VC.

Any further German advance was now out of the question. The darkness, together with hedges and wire fences, prevented any thoughts of overwhelming the Guards, who in reality were never seriously threatened. 'So the night

An artist's impression of the rearguard at Landrecies, giving a rather false impression of the intensity of the fighting.

wore on with bursts of rapid fire at intervals, one of the longest nights I have ever spent,' wrote Bernard Gordon Lennox. At first light it became obvious that the Germans had withdrawn and soon after came the order for the Guards to begin evacuating the town. The place was in a mess and the last of the civilian population had long gone:

> *The streets had been barricaded through the night with every conceivable sort of thing, carts wagons and faggots and all available paraphernalia. Unfortunately we had no time to get our kits, the men having turned out in such a hurry, and they had to be left behind.*

The Irish Guards had been responsible for the barricades and Lieutenant Aubrey Herbert, although still the Member of Parliament for Yeovil, had managed to wangle himself a commission in the Irish Guards and leave for France as the official interpreter with the 1st Battalion. Although the time he gives is probably incorrect, he describes the confusion in the town as 4 Guards Brigade was preparing to leave:

Lieutenant Aubrey Herbert continued as MP for Yeovil during his war service.

> *About 2.30, in my sleep I heard my name, and found Desmond* [Captain Lord Desmond FitzGerald] *calling me loudly in the street outside. He said: 'We have lost two young officers ... Come out and find them at once. The Germans are coming into the town, and we shall have to clear out instantly'. I said to him: 'I don't know either* [of them] *by sight, and if I did it is far too dark to see them.' 'Well,' he said, 'You must do your best.' I went out and walked about the town, which was still being shelled, but I was far more afraid of being run over in the darkness than of being hit. Troops were pouring out in great confusion – foot, artillery, transport mixed – and there were great holes in the road made by the German shells.*

The two officers in question were Second Lieutenants Woodroffe and Livingstone-Learmonth, neither of whom were located by Aubrey Herbert in his rather half hearted attempt to find them. They were in fact sleeping, having failed to hear the call to arms and eventually woke in daylight with the battalion long gone and the Germans in the town. Fortunately they fell into the hands of one of the captured RAMC officers, who by chance knew the whereabouts of a horse abandoned by one of the British battalions. Seizing their opportunity, the two young officers mounted the steed and managed to escape across country. Second Lieutenant Neville Woodroffe later wrote home about the incident:

> *My personal billet was away from my own platoon as I and another officer had managed to find a room in another part of the village in which to sleep. However, when the alarm went we did not hear it and the two men detailed to warn us never came so eventually when the remainder had managed to get out of the place we were left asleep in our room. We woke up at 7 o'clock and found the town surrounded by Germans and the village partly blown down. The house next to ours was completely shattered and all windows and roofs of the neighbouring houses were smashed and the streets torn up. We collected our kit and made out as quickly as possible.*

Marching with the Guards Brigade away from Landrecies were two officers and seventy other ranks of 19/Field Ambulance. The remaining sections of 19/Field Ambulance, who had marched into Landrecies at 5.00pm the previous day, now set about transferring the less severely wounded to the waiting ambulance train. One of those was Robert Whitbread:

> *Hawarden* [Lieutenant R C Hawarden] *was in the next bed to me and was quite cheerful in spite of very bad wounds. He afterwards died I regret to say. I should think it was about 8am on the 26th when one of the medical officers came round telling all who could walk or hobble to go outside as a fresh lot of wounded had just been brought in. I got into an ambulance and with a lot of other ambulances went to Guise.*

Lieutenant Robert Cornwallis Maude, 6th Viscount Hawarden.

Whitbread was one of the more fortunate wounded who were evacuated before the Germans arrived. Not so for the men of 4/Field Ambulance, who now resigned themselves to the inevitable and began the task of treating the wounded and burying the dead. They had been directed to

Landrecies with I Corps, having spent much of the day treating exhausted men in the wake of the main columns. They arrived just east of the town soon after the action began and sensibly halted in an orchard, along with several stragglers from 13/Field Ambulance. When the Germans entered the town some hours later, 4/Field Ambulance and two sections of 19/Field Ambulance were taken prisoner. It is interesting to note that the casualty figures reported by *IR 27* – thirty seven killed and eighty eight wounded – concurs with the evidence of two of the captured RAMC officers, who found only thirty new German graves, a long way short of the 800 dead Germans that Brigadier General Scott-Kerr reported in his account of the incident!

Of the British casualties, the greater number were from the Coldstream Guards, who left twelve dead and seven missing when they retired. Of the 105 wounded, evidence from Private Joseph Taylor, who was captured with one of the field ambulances, suggests only thirty of them were left behind at Landrecies. The Grenadiers lost Second Lieutenant Robert Vereker, who was killed fighting with Bernard Gordon Lennox's company, together with six NCOs and men wounded.

Although he remained at Landrecies until 11.30pm that evening, Douglas Haig soon moved his HQ to the nearby village of Le Grand Fayt under the impression that his I Corps were in grave danger of being overrun. If we are to accept his own account, he and his Chief of Staff, Johnnie Gough, place much of the blame for what he describes as the 'penetration' of the town's defences on the 'sleepy' Guards and his diary gives the impression he personally directed operations until he left for the security of 3 Brigade HQ at Le Grand Fayt. Haig was clearly rattled by this surprise attack and his report to GHQ, now even further south at St Quentin, that he was under assault by four German divisions caused some consternation amongst an already anxious staff. Even at 3.50am on the 26th, when he was six miles away from the fighting, he requested further assistance from Smith-Dorrien, suggesting that troops at Le Cateau should immediately advance to Landrecies. But Smith-Dorrien was preoccupied with the forthcoming Battle of Le Cateau and failed to respond.

To be fair, in defence of Haig's apparent panic, it could be argued that the quite disproportionate amount of firing which was kept up until daybreak at Landrecies and the uncertainty of the number of the enemy that might be hidden in the Forêt de Mormal was reason enough for Haig's alarm. Indeed, had Haig and his staff been taken prisoner it would have been a major coup for the Germans and one that would have perhaps altered the whole course of the war. Nevertheless and more importantly perhaps – from the troops' point of view – it had the unfortunate result of keeping the Guards Brigade under arms all night and depriving the weary troops of their much needed rest.

With Haig assuming the worst and GHQ appearing to believe I Corps was under a sustained attack, questions were being asked as to why Haig had decided to halt on the Landrecies line and not east of Le Cateau as ordered. While Haig claims he received the approval of GHQ, Henry Wilson appears to refute this and was of the opinion that he should be 'made to go on to Le Cateau' otherwise there would 'be an awkward gap'. Whether Haig, with his increasing distrust of Sir John French's ability to support I Corps, decided to beat his own course and ignore GHQ's directives can only be left to conjecture; but he did choose to ignore an order directing him to rejoin II Corps the next day at Busigny, some seven miles southwest of Le Cateau.

The Rearguard Action at Maroilles 25 August 1918

The attack on Landrecies was made by the advance guard of the German *7th Division*, which had marched along the western side of the Forest, quite unaware that the town was occupied by the British. The attack on Maroilles was made under similar circumstances by the advance guard of the German *5th Division*, which had marched through the Forest. In the space of nine days the inhabitants of both towns had witnessed the BEF marching north in expectation of victory and then returning in disarray with the Germans in hot pursuit. Maroilles on the evening of 25 August was an entirely different place to that experienced earlier in the month by Cyril Helm, the Medical Officer attached to 2/KOYLI. When

The Machine Gun Section of 2nd Battalion KOSB at Maroilles on their way to Mons on 20 August.

he arrived on 16 August the battalion had spent 'two happy days' being billeted on local farms and people 'gave them as much butter and milk as they wanted'. Now the single main street of the small town was choked with refugees and military transports, causing some consternation to Lieutenant Alan Hanbury-Sparrow, the transport officer of 1st Battalion Royal Berkshire Regiment, who had just turned up with the battalion after a fourteen mile march from Bavay along some extremely congested roads:

Lieutenant Alan Hanbury-Sparrow.

Wherever you look you can see wagons, carts and pedestrians making for the road you are on. The whole countryside is emptying itself onto it. The little groups you behold are rivulets hastening to join the main stream on the road, which soon becomes a spate of refugees, pouring along like a highland torrent.

The Berkshires had spent the previous night in a cornfield and had been detailed as brigade rearguard on 25 August. Being the last to arrive, they were looking forward in typically soldierly fashion to getting something to eat and a place to get their heads down for a couple of hours. B Squadron, 15/Hussars had been with the battalion on and off for most of the day, with several small detachments patrolling the numerous rides which criss-crossed the forest. Leaving the Berkshires at Pont-sur-Sambre, the squadron trotted on to Noyelles, where they were to be billeted. No sooner had they dismounted and loosened the girths of their weary horses, than orders arrived to occupy the bridges at Maroilles and remain in position until relieved by the infantry.

Captain the Hon William Nugent arrived at the Hachette Bridge, north west of Maroilles, just as it was getting dark. The Forêt de Mormal came almost down to the banks of the Sambre at this point and there was very little the hussars could do to fortify the crossing apart from defend the approach road between the railway crossing and the river and put a troop on the bridge itself. The second, smaller bridge, was further down the canal to the east of Maroilles and here Nugent sent Lieutenant Guy Straker and his troop. With the sounds of heavy firing coming from the direction of Landrecies, Nugent realised he would probably soon be under attack himself. He was not wrong as at 8.00pm the first units of the German *III Army Corps* attacked Nugent's bridge, bringing up artillery to fire directly at the besieged cavalrymen. They hung on

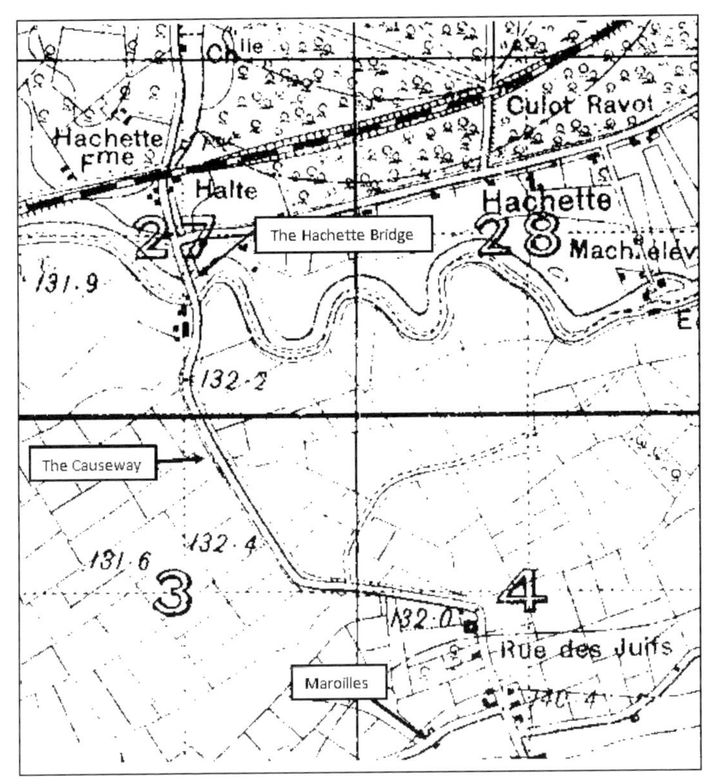

A contemporary 1914 map of the Hachette bridge north of Maroilles showing the line of the causeway. The modern D32 had not been constructed in 1914.

grimly until the weight of fire forced them to abandon the bridge to the enemy. Realising Lieutenant Straker's bridge was now in danger, Private William Price slipped into the canal and swam down to Straker, warning him of the danger. Straker was able to withdraw his troop before he was surrounded and Price was awarded the DCM for his bravery.

As soon as the attack on the bridge began, Nugent sent a galloper to Maroilles with a request for help; halfway along the raised causeway that ran back towards Maroilles he met a company of the Berkshires en route to the bridge. By this time, according to German sources, the hussars had been forced back towards Maroilles and the advance units were marching towards the town. As Major Alexander Turner and B Company were doubling up the causeway, he and his men discovered from the hussars that they had been driven off the bridge, which was now occupied by German infantry. The German account reports a skirmish on the causeway between the two opposing sides that resulted

The bridge over the Sambre at Hachette.

in a German retirement to the bridge in the face of what they described as superior forces. However, despite several sources giving accounts of the engagement that followed, there is still a fog of uncertainty as to exactly what did take place.

The *Official History* tells us that B Company 'took post by the Rue des Juifs, about a mile to the southeast of the bridge.' Turner was then enticed forward by some troops on the bridge who appeared to be French, where he was wounded and taken prisoner. Quite why this encounter took place when the hussars had already pulled back from the bridge under fire is a mystery but two accounts of the death of Captain Henry Shott in his service record do throw a little more light on what took place after Turner's capture.

Henry Shott was highly regarded by his men and considered to be one of the bravest in the battalion; the fact that he began his military career in South Africa as a trooper in Bethune's Mounted Infantry doubtlessly endeared him to the men under his command. He was commissioned in 1900 and his award of the DSO was announced in the *London Gazette* in 1902. Promotion to captain came in 1911, followed three years later by his marriage to Hazel Brown, five weeks before he left for France. She was never to see her husband again. According to evidence given by Sergeant John Frogley, when the company was advancing along the causeway to take the bridge:

Captain Henry Shott.

Captain Shott went to the left of the bridge and swam the River Sambre, returned and collected some men, including myself, returned again to the river, a fierce fire fight being opened upon us. Captain Shott again entered the river. On orders to retire from the position, Captain Shott had not returned.

Rather frustratingly, Frogley's account does not go onto say what happened next. If this took place after Turner had been captured, which in all probability it did, Shott was either attempting a rescue bid or trying to establish a presence on the northern end of the bridge. This is borne out to some extent by Private Watts, who states in his account that B Company were holding the bridge at the time of Shott's death. Turner's own account of what occurred after his capture speaks of a 'fusillade [of shots] that broke out from our side of the river [it must have been the battalion attacking the bridgehead] and several bullets passing through the wall of the stable', where he was being held. Was this in reality Captain Shott's attempt at rescue? We will never know. Thus the situation when the remainder of the battalion arrived was: B Company, less two of its senior officers, in shaky possession of the causeway and one end of the bridge and the Germans holding the remainder.

The arrival of two further companies of Berkshires and a charge across the bridge led by Lieutenant Charles Fulbrook-Legatt and Major Herbert Finch secured the southern end of the bridge after some close quarter fighting, resulting in many of the wounded falling down the steep banks of the causeway and drowning. Drummer Henry Savage was one of those who was floundering in deep water and was rescued by Corporal Walter Brindle. Brindle rescued a number of men from a watery death before he was killed by a shell.

The Berkshires' war diary for 25 August records the action at the bridge with ten short lines but it does state the 'bridge was taken about 1.30 after a night attack by B, D and C Companies'. This is unlikely, given the weight of opposition and the presence of a German artillery piece positioned to fire directly along the line of the bridge. However, Private Wright, who was fighting with C Company, is sure they retook the bridge. His account, although a little garbled, does point to more than one attempt to retake the bridge:

Then came the most exciting part of the evening, namely the charging and retaking of the bridge. I don't think any of us who took part will ever forget that. For my part I seem to have gone mad. My ears ringing with the noise of the firing and cheering. I did find myself on the bridge in the second charge, there wasn't many of us, about 40 of us, no more until the work was finished, then many more.

But whatever happened on that wet and dark night, by holding the bridge until the 1st Battalion King's Royal Rifle Corps arrived to relieve them, the Berkshires prevented the enemy advancing on Maroilles and allowed the overcrowded and congested main street in the town to clear itself, much to the relief of Lieutenant Hanbury-Sparrow

The Rearguard Action at Le Grand Fayt – 26 August 1914

I Corps was now marching south but on a parallel course to Smith-Dorrien and further to the east, towards Guise. Its route would widen the gap between the two commands and bring it into further contact with von Bülow's *Second Army*. Over the next forty eight hours that contact would strike two heavy blows, the first of which would be centred on the village of Le Grand Fayt, whence Douglas Haig had fled in the early hours of 26 August after the Landrecies attack. Dubbed the 'Rearguard Affair of Le Grand Fayt' in the *Official History*, it serves to illustrate the penalties of poor command and control, which resulted in many men being scattered far and wide and condemned many more to weeks and even months of hiding behind enemy lines – sometimes with fatal results.

In order to fully appreciate what happened at Le Grand Fayt it is necessary to return to 25 August. Readers will recall that Douglas Haig

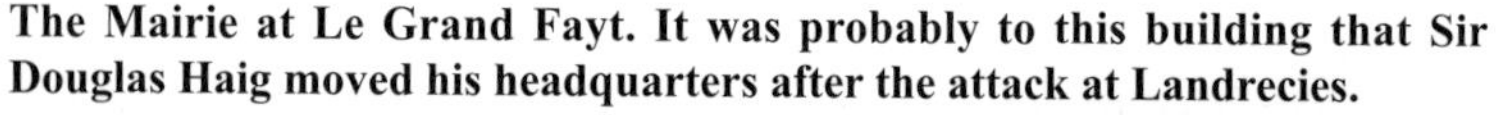

The Mairie at Le Grand Fayt. It was probably to this building that Sir Douglas Haig moved his headquarters after the attack at Landrecies.

had moved his headquarters to Le Grand Fayt after the Landrecies attack to join Brigadier General Herman Landon and 3 Brigade, which had been in billets there since 6.30pm that evening. The 3 Brigade war diaries for 25 August provide us with an impression of the bedlam that greeted the men as they arrived in that hitherto small and tranquil settlement:

Brigadier General Herman Landon, GOC 3 Brigade. Landon had his headquarters at the Mairie at Grand Fayt.

> *There are crowds of wretched people on foot and in carts, going south all over the place. Brigade left Marbaix, except Queen's* [Royal West Surrey Regiment] *who had preceded it, and reached Le Grand Fayt. Here, what with the "Convoie Administrative" of the 53rd Division de Reserve, the Heavy Battery and Divisional Ammunition Column of the 2nd Division all coming in the opposite direction to assemble, there was a pretty good muddle.*

Contributing to the muddle was the 1st Battalion Gloucestershire Regiment (1/Gloucesters). Even by today's standards, given the size of the village, quite where everyone was accommodated in 1914 is a mystery but at least C Company of 1/Gloucesters passed a relatively undisturbed night on outpost duties on the outskirts of the village, listening to the machine gun and rifle fire coming from the Landrecies and Maroilles actions. A little before midnight Douglas Haig's motor cavalcade had driven into the crowded village, announcing his arrival and that of his staff; an event which hopefully did not catch the outpost commander by surprise. Having conferred with General Landon, and still convinced that he had a large force of German infantry hot on his heels, Haig ordered the 1st Division to move immediately and take up a position near Favil to cover the withdrawal of the 2nd Division.

Haig's fresh orders for the next day's retirement took some time to percolate down to the 2nd Division's brigade commanders who, in turn, had to send word to their subordinates in command of battalions. It was, therefore, not until sometime after 4.00am on 26 August that Brigadier General Richard Haking, the officer commanding 5 Brigade, was able to get a message to Lieutenant Colonel Alexander Abercrombie and the 2nd Battalion Connaught Rangers (2/Connaught Rangers) who were at Noyelles, directing him to act as rearguard to the brigade. Haking's brigade was at the most northerly extremity of I Corps and thus, in effect, the Connaught Rangers would be acting as rearguard to the entire division.

1/Gloucesters marched out of Le Grand Fayt at 5.00am – almost exactly an hour later than Abercrombie's Connaught Rangers, who left their billets at Noyelles, some five miles further north, at 4.00am. Marching south west across country, the Gloucesters soon reached Favil and sent a patrol from A Company out towards Landrecies whilst the remainder of the battalion positioned itself as rearguard across the main Landrecies road, close to two guns of 54/Battery. These guns, under section commander Lieutenant Ralph Blewitt, came into action shortly after noon when a German column was seen on the western bank of the Sambre Canal. German artillery responded with alacrity and, although the majority of shells fell short, several men in C Company were wounded. German shooting was very much improved after an aeroplane in French colours – which later transpired to be German – flew low over the Gloucesters' trenches. Soon after the aircraft had passed over them, a German infantry attack developed from the direction of Landrecies, forcing the Gloucesters to withdraw B Company from its advanced position 200 yards up the road. The first two fatalities of the war to be suffered by the battalion were inflicted during this withdrawal, one of which, Private James Lander, was seriously wounded when he was caught up in close-quarter fighting during the forced withdrawal of his company. The 35 year old reservist died of his wounds the next day at Landrecies and was buried by a party of 4/Field Ambulance, which had remained behind with the wounded of the Guards Brigade. Lander's company commander, Captain Guy Shipway, was hit by sniper fire in the same action and later died of his wounds at Étreux . By 5.00pm the excitement was all but over. German forces, not wishing to get too enmeshed with troops of 3 Brigade, withdrew, giving the Gloucesters time to disengage and get clear.

In the intervening period a semblance of

Lieutenant Colonel Alexander Abercrombie commanded the 2nd Battalion Connaught Rangers.

Captain Guy Shipway was the first officer of the Gloucestershire Regiment to be killed in action during the Great War.

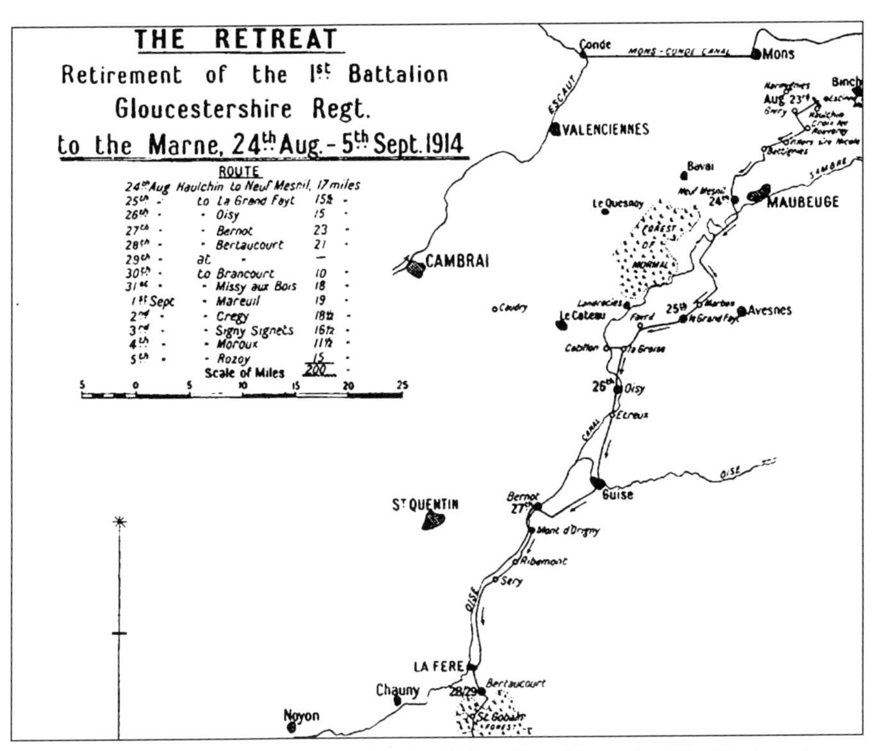

Part of the line of retreat taken by the 1st Battalion Gloucestershire Regiment from Mons. Note the relentless daily march statistics, with only one day of rest, on 29 August.

composure had returned to Le Grand Fayt and, apart from the occasional troop of French cavalry passing through, the village was left relatively undisturbed. Unfortunately this proved to be the calm before the storm. A few miles to the north the march of the Connaught Rangers from Noyelles had been uninterrupted and, on arriving at Taisnières-en-Thiérache, B Company moved to the crossroads south of the village whilst the remaining three companies followed the main column to Marbaix, where the road crosses the main Maroilles-Avesnes road. Here the brigade transport was held up by a large French force of territorials moving east. Anticipating a long wait, Colonel Abercrombie ordered A Company to remain with the transport and sent C and D Companies to the crossroads south of Taisnières, where they were briefly reunited with B Company.

At the crossroads they met detachments of French cavalry, which informed them that there were no Germans in the vicinity. Accordingly, Abercrombie sent word to Brigade HQ that he would remain in position until 3.00pm and then march to Le Grand Fayt. A view of the situation from the ranks is provided by Sergeant John McIlwain, a reservist who had been called up in early August and was then serving as a platoon sergeant in D Company. His account gives an insight into the very slow progress made by the battalion that morning. They had been on the march for several hours but McIlwain apparently had no idea what they were supposed to be doing: 'Told to keep a sharp lookout for Uhlans. We appeared to be on some covering movement. No rations this day. Seemed to be cut off from supplies. Slept again for an hour or so on a sloping road until 11am.'

The battalion war diary does not indicate the time the battalion arrived at the crossroads but from all accounts it must have been there for some time if John McIlwain's diary is anywhere near accurate. 'We retired to a field, were told we could drum-up as we had tea. I went to a nearby village to get bread. None to be had, but got a fine drink of milk and some pears'.

At 3.00pm Captain Ernest Hamilton and A Company entered Le Grand Fayt and, according to Hamilton's account, set about organizing billets for the battalion at the request of Colonel Abercrombie! Back at the crossroads at 3.15pm firing was heard coming from the direction of Marbaix, quickly followed by French cavalry galloping helter-skelter up the road and shouting that 200 Germans with a machine gun were close by. Reacting to this threat personally, Abercrombie led about 100 men from C and D Companies up the road towards Marbaix, where they almost immediately came under heavy enemy fire, forcing them to seek cover on the high ground to the south. It appears the colonel left no orders with Major William Alexander and Captain O'Sullivan, who remained at the crossroads with the remainder of the two companies.

German horse artillery such as these opened fire on the crossroads south of Taisnières and Le Grand Fayt.

Shortly after Abercrombie had moved off towards Marbaix, the crossroads became the focus of German horse artillery shell fire, as did the village of Le Grand Fayt. Fortunately, 5 Brigade transport had passed through but, as Ernest Hamilton observed, 'in five minutes what had appeared to be a peaceful hamlet became a positive inferno'. Expecting an imminent infantry attack, Hamilton tried to reach Abercrombie but found the road blocked by German troops. He then took the only sensible option open to him and marched south west towards Étreux, arriving there at 11.00pm. Hamilton had vivid memories of that night march, which he later described in the regimental history:

> *I could not ride my horse as I fell asleep the moment I got up. I even fell asleep walking – to be awakened by bumping into the men in front of me, most of whom were also half asleep. Some of them fell out and lay down in the road – it exhausted all one's vocabulary of entreaty and abuse, and even called for a liberal use of the boot to get them up again. Even so, in spite of our efforts, I am afraid some half dozen were left behind.*

In the meantime Colonel Abercrombie sent Second Lieutenant Robert Benison down to the village to inform Brigade HQ that he was under attack. Benison returned with the disconcerting news that the 5 Brigade staff had left the village and it was apparently deserted and under fire. The battalion was now scattered widely and none of the battalion's senior officers appeared to be in possession of their commanding officer's plan of action. Thus at this critical point in the proceedings the situation was as follows: Abercrombie with five officers, including the battalion second in command, Major William Sarsfield and about a hundred men, were under fire on the high ground to the north of Le Grand Fayt. A Company was marching south with the brigade transport – as was B Company with Major Hugh Hutchinson, who, after failing to get in touch with Colonel Abercrombie, decided to follow the transport – whilst the remainder of C and D Companies were still at the crossroads just south of Taisnières.

Up at the crossroads, Major Alexander – still unsure of the whereabouts of A and B Companies – now faced a dilemma: should he wait for Abercrombie, whom he presumed was somewhere further east responding to the enemy fire, or should he proceed to Le Grand Fayt in the hope that he would find the remainder of the battalion there? Bearing in mind the crossroads was being shelled and he was taking casualties, his decision to move downhill to the by now shell-torn village was, in the event, a most reasonable one. John McIlwain provides a glimpsc of the uncertainty and confusion that prevailed at the time. He was at the crossroads when he and his comrades first came under shell fire:

> *Then the Germans got the range of us ... and it simply rained small shells, horse artillery apparently. I followed my platoon officer, Lieutenant* [Second Lieutenant Victor] *Lentaigne into a turnip field. When taking cover, Private* [Patrick] *Sweeney, an old Indian wallah, lying beside me was wounded. Had to cut our way through a hedge to help Sweeney onto the road. Formed up under our company commander, Major Alexander. Cut off from the remainder of the battalion. Major at a loss.*

Collecting as many men as they could, Alexander and O'Sullivan moved into Le Grand Fayt sometime after 6.00pm to find French troops about to retire. The French officer in command had no idea where Colonel Abercrombie might be, but recommended immediate retirement as they were all in danger of being overrun by a large force of German cavalry and motorized infantry. Mcllwain was part of the advance guard as they retired towards Beaurepaire:

> *I, with eight men, do advance guard. Fixed bayonets and a sharp lookout each side of the road, but still no Germans. After sundown came up with some French troops in a village* [probably Cartignies] *they had retired to, chased by Germans. Germans a mile or so behind us, burning the village as they pass. The sky lit up. Then rain, rain! And I, in the stress of the retreat, like so many others who were trained by Kitchener always to travel light, had thrown away my great coat.*

Their march ended at Le Nouvion at midnight where, soaking wet through and exhausted, they bivouacked a mile south of the town.

So what of Colonel Abercrombie and his party? After coming under fire near Marbaix and realizing Brigade HQ was no longer at Le Grand Fayt, he and his party continued their retirement downhill towards the village. The country above Le Grand Fayt is difficult to move through, and thick hedges and numerous orchards – which largely remain today – made communication and movement difficult. Together with Lieutenant Gordon Barker's machine gun section, Abercrombie deployed 33 year old Captain Francis Leader and Second Lieutenant Charles Turner with a platoon from D Company as rearguard. Abercrombie had only just moved off towards the village when the rearguard party came under

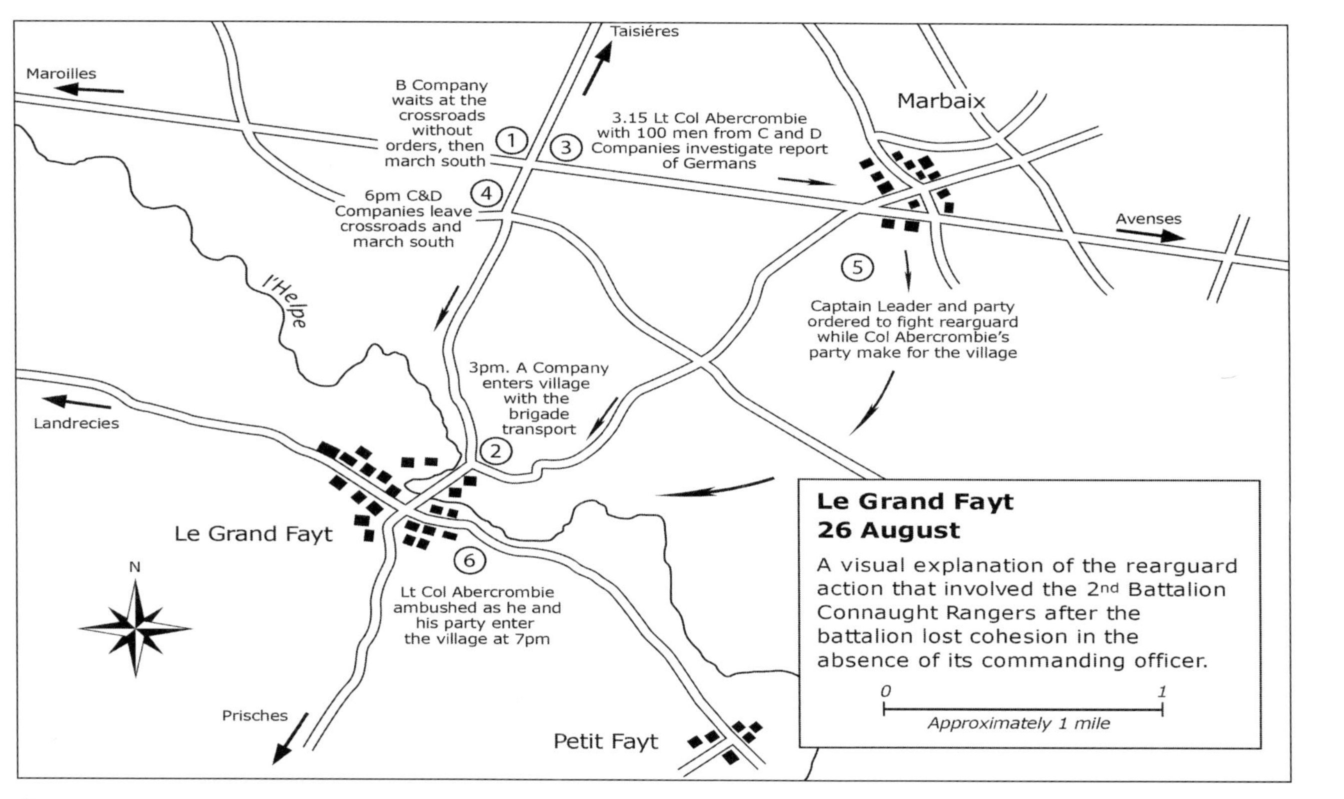

The rearguard action at Grand Fayt was an unnecessary encounter that should not have really taken place at all. A question remains over Lieutenant Colonel Abercrombie's actions on the day and that of his brigade commander, Brigadier General Richard Haking.

heavy attack. Captain Leader, with little choice but to hold on as long as possible, was in a poorly placed position lining the side of one of the small minor roads running down to the village from the Maroilles-Marbaix road. As the night drew on ammunition became short.

Charles Turner and four men were alongside Gordon Barker and the machine gun section and it soon became apparent to both officers that they were up against a much larger force than first realized and that their situation was rapidly becoming indefensible. Just after dusk, outgunned and enfiladed, Captain Leader was killed. Barker fired the last round from the one remaining machine gun and took charge of the few men that remained. Ordering them to fix bayonets, he led them in a last counter attack. The gallant young officer was brought down by a bullet in the thigh and Charles Turner was hit twice in the shoulder, leaving him dazed and only partly conscious:

Private Egerton Emerson (pictured on the left) was taken prisoner at Le Grand Fayt. His younger brother, Second Lieutenant James Emerson, won a posthumous VC for his bravery in December 1917.

> *I only collected my senses in time to see the forms of men looming up in front, whom I knew by their voices to be Germans. Some of them showed a decided inclination to bayonet me, but they were ordered off by a German officer, who immediately knelt down beside me and asked why we were fighting against them, also various questions as to the strength of our force, to all of which I professed ignorance.*

They were fortunate that Barker spoke German fluently, which seemed to 'command our captors' respect at once'. Turner's belongings, which had been taken from him earlier, were duly returned after Barker spoke to the officer and who 'appeared to dress down the enlisted German soldiers in very sharp tones'. The survivors spent the night in the field and were taken the next morning in a cart to Avenses-sur-Helpe. By rights Barker should have been decorated for his gallantry that night but he died of his injuries in England in December 1916 after being repatriated and the story of what took place above Le Grand Fayt remained forgotten until long after the war was over.

Meanwhile the Connaught Rangers, led by Abercrombie, Captain Walter Roche, Major Sarsfield and Lieutenants de Stacpoole and Hardy, approached the village at about 7.00pm. Told by an inhabitant that there were no German forces in the village, the Rangers were ambushed minutes later by a strong force of Germans hidden on either side of the road. Pandemonium prevailed as officers and men scattered in all directions, Major Sarsfield and Robert de Stacpoole succeeded in escaping through the village with a handful of men and eventually rejoined the battalion, where Sarsfield assumed command of it. Tragically, he was killed on the Aisne a matter of weeks later. Colonel Abercrombie, with Captain Roche and Jocelyn Hardy, gathered up some fifty men and also got through the village, taking up a defensive position to the west near Le Gard, where they again came under fire. For some unexplained reason Abercrombie then headed northwest instead of south. Had he moved south he might have evaded capture and been reunited with the battalion.

Lieutenant Jocelyn Hardy was taken prisoner at Maroilles but eventually escaped back to England.

On the word of a local man that there were still English troops at Maroilles, Abercrombie led his party in that direction and before long was met by Lieutenant Colonel Thompson, the Assistant Director of Medical

The Mairie and school house at Maroilles. This was one of the two buildings in which Colonel Abercrombie and his party were eventually discovered by German troops after the Le Grand Fayt episode.

Services for the 2nd Division, who was about to evacuate the town with a field ambulance convoy. He directed the Connaught Rangers to the two houses which had been used as field hospitals – one of which was the local school. English troops, he thought, were due to be back in Maroilles the next morning. Thompson then left to rejoin the field ambulance but lost his horse in the darkness; stumbling into the village of Prisches, he was captured the next morning just after the *curé* had presented him with three Connaught Rangers he had found hiding in the church.

General Mordecai Valabrègue commanded the reserve divisions of the French Fifth Army. It was units from his divisions that initially held up the Connaught Rangers on 26 August.

Bad luck still continued to haunt the luckless Abercrombie. Hardly had the Rangers got inside the two buildings pointed out by Thompson than German troops entered Maroilles. Remaining quiet, they were undetected until the next day, when Abercrombie's party was discovered early in the morning and taken into captivity. For a short while it looked as if Captain Roche's group would remain hidden but their luck ran out at 7.00pm that evening when they were finally discovered and made prisoner.

With the loss of six officers and 280 other ranks in an encounter that should never really have taken place, questions inevitably arise as to the effectiveness of Lieutenant Colonel Abercrombie's handling of the situation. True, the battalion was held up by General Valabrègue's reserve divisions on the Mariolles-Marbaix road south of Taisnières, which did allow the vanguard of von Richtofen's *Guard Cavalry* to make contact; but should Abercrombie have taken personal command of the force he sent forward in response to gunfire from the Marbaix direction? Would it perhaps not have been better to have despatched one of his company commanders to assess the situation whilst the remainder of the battalion continued on into Le Grand Fayt, rather than allow two companies to rest for several hours at the crossroads – apparently without orders? Unfortunately Abercrombie's version of the episode went with him into captivity, during which he died in November 1915 and it was forever lost. Young Charles Turner was invalided first to Switzerland and then eventually to England, whilst the irrepressible Jocelyn Hardy made nine escape attempts until he finally succeeded in making a home run in 1918.

Stage 2

Étreux to Cerizy

In this section we cover the rearguard action on 27 August which began north of the town at the Chapeau Rouge crossroads and concluded at Étreux with the last stand of the remaining officers and men of the 2nd Royal Munster Fusiliers. We then move south of St Quentin to Cerizy, where 5 Cavalry Brigade fought a classic rearguard action in the shallow valley near La Guinguette Farm on 28 August.

Background

The retirement route taken by I Corps on 27 August included the large village of Étreux before it moved south of Guise to the high ground. The rearguard for the day was the responsibility of Brigadier General Ivor Maxse who, on hearing that practically the whole of Haig's Corps was to use the same highway to Guise, realized that the day 'promised to be critical'. I Corps was underway by 4.00am, with the 1st Division remaining in a covering position until the 2nd Division had moved off. By 7.00am Maxse had moved his brigade headquarters from Fesmy to the canal bridge at Petit Cambrésis, where he was visited by his divisional commander, Major General Samuel Lomax, who made it clear that it was vital to hold the Fesmy-Wassigny line until the two divisions of I Corps had passed through Étreux. Not only were they passing through, reiterated Lomax, but they were being resupplied in the town and thus it was essential that this took place unhindered. Accordingly, Maxse issued his orders: the first to 23/Field Company and Lieutenant Colonel Adrian Grant-Duff of 1/Black Watch, to reconnoitre and prepare a fall-back rearguard position just north of Étreux . His second batch of orders were issued to the three rearguard units, which consisted of: 2/Munsters, with the addition of C Squadron 15/Hussars under Major Frederick Pilkington and C and D Guns from 118/Battery, XXVI Brigade, in the charge of Major Abingdon Bayly.

Brigadier General Ivor Maxse commanded 1 Guards Brigade on 27 August 1914.

The Munster's deployment

Major Paul Charrier, the commanding officer of the 2nd Battalion Royal Munster Fusiliers.

Commanding the Munsters was Major Paul Alfred Charrier, a man fluent in French and very much a Francophile, who had joined the battalion in 1890. Known in the regiment as an individualist, the 45 year old Charrier was easy to spot on the march in his brown tropical issue pith helmet with its green and white hackle of Munster, a nostalgic reminder perhaps for those with an eye for the history of the regiment's origins under Clive of India in 1756. Mentioned in despatches in 1901 for service in West Africa, he went on to serve with the Imperial Yeomanry during the Boer War.

Major Charrier prepared his defensive positions with B and D Companies at the Chapeau Rouge crossroads and A Company less two platoons at Bergues-sur-Sambre. C Company and Charrier's HQ were at Fesmy-le-Sart. Contact with German forces that morning had begun early in the day; shortly after dawn the 15/Hussars found themselves deployed right across the brigade frontage, with a strong detachment at Chapeau Rouge and another with the Munsters at Fesmy. German forces were evidently moving quickly.

As the tail end of the long and weary column of men and equipment passed through the Munsters' lines on their way south, the 1st Battalion Coldstream Guards (1/Coldstream) left two of their companies on the left of the main Landrecies road – the D946 – to defend the bridge over the Sambre Canal just north of Petit Cambrésis. By 10.00am, with the sky darkening to the north and threatening rain, most of the 15/Hussars' patrols had been forced back and thick lines of infantry of the German *X Corps*, many of whom had been brought forward in motor lorries, were advancing across the fields on both flanks. At the Chapeau Rouge crossroads B and D Companies of 2/Munsters were engaged in a furious fire fight at close quarters. In the confusion which followed – aided by the rain, which was now sheeting down in torrents – the two companies withdrew, D Company down the Bergues road towards Fesmy and B Company, under the command of Captain George Simms, towards Oisy. Those German units which had come up against Charrier's positions in the village had waited until they were in enough strength to penetrate Fesmy, but a counter attack by Captain Claud Rawlinson and C Company cleared the village and restored the status quo for the time being. It was now 1.00pm.

The message from General Maxse, which went out at 12.46pm,

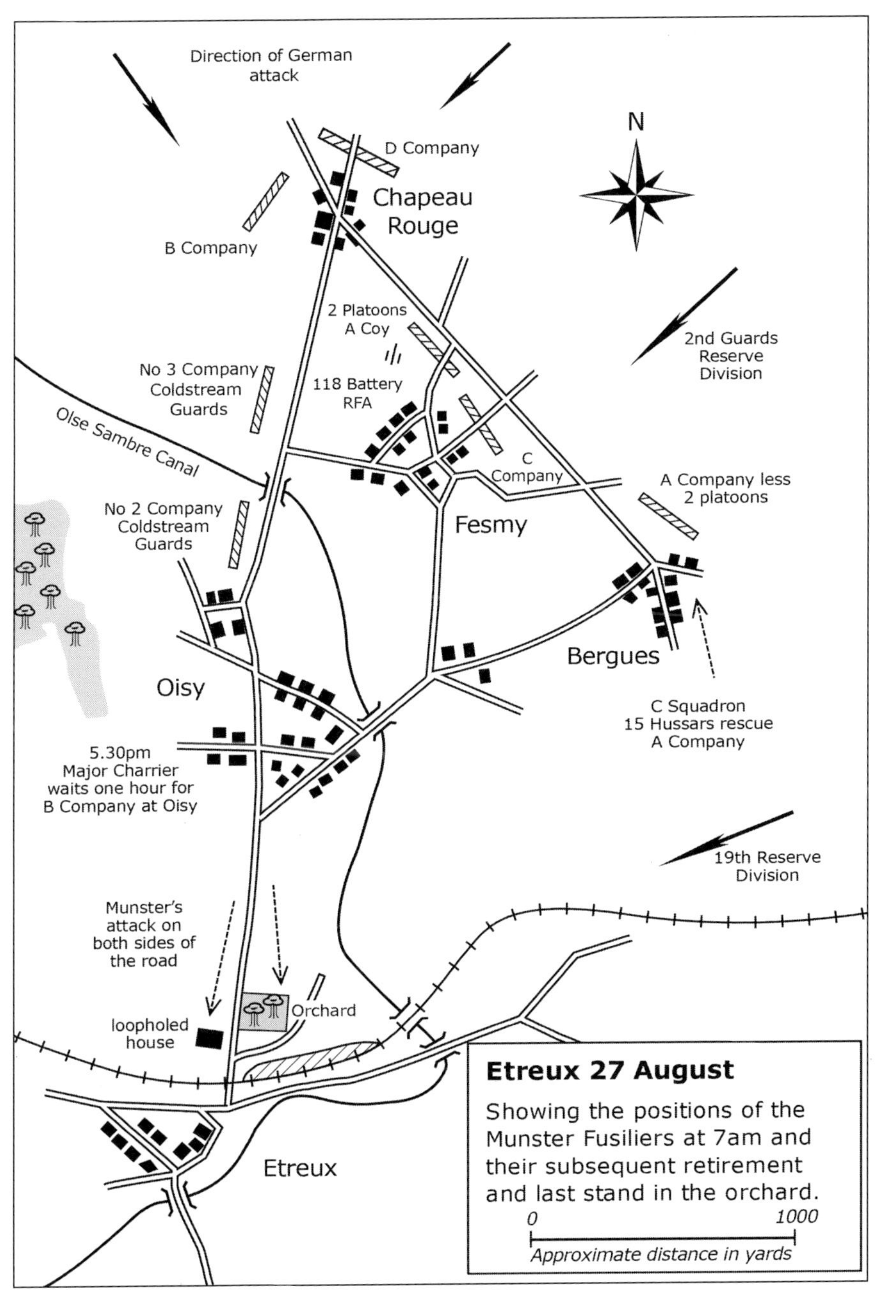

The Munsters' rearguard on 27 August began at Chapeau Rouge and concluded in the orchard just north of Etreux.

ordering all rearguard units to retire, did not reach Charrier at his battalion headquarters at Fesmy. The cyclist carrying those orders came under fire north of Petit Cambrésis and was unable to reach the Munsters, whilst further attempts to get through to Charrier on horseback were unsuccessful. However, the orders did get through to Captain John Gibbs and the two Coldstream companies, which withdrew to the bridge and continued their march south through Étreux.

At Fesmy Major Charrier was under a sustained attack, leaving him with little alternative but to begin his retirement towards Étreux. At 3.00pm the Munsters were in the process of pulling back towards Oisy when Charrier got word that German cavalry had been seen to the south. It was an ominous sign that the enemy was closing in.

Rescue at Bergues-sur-Sambre

With German infantry reported to be in the wooded area south of Boué, the danger of becoming surrounded was fast becoming a reality. There was now only one gap in the enveloping circle of German units and that was at Bergues-sur-Sambre. In conference with Major Pilkington, Ivor Maxse ordered the 15/Hussars to attempt a rescue. The 'greater part of the squadron therefore dashed for this gap and a fierce fight now ensued

The 15th King's Hussars, seen here before the outbreak of war, were able to exploit the rescue corridor for the Munsters of A Company, who were at Bergues-sur-Sambre.

at the outskirts of Bergues'. Pilkington's men attacked with such determination that the Germans were caught a little off guard and in the ensuing mêlée over 170 men of the Munsters retired under the covering fire of the Hussars. It was a gallant action but it was not without cost. In enabling the Munsters to get away relatively unscathed, Private William Wilkes was killed in action and Lance Corporal John Stent died of his wounds six months later in captivity at Guise. The only officer to fall in the action was Lieutenant the Hon Edward Charles Hardinge, who was wounded in both arms and later died of his wounds in England. But for the vast majority of the remaining men of Charrier's battalion and the gunners of 118/Battery there would be no escape as they moved south to Étreux .

Oisy crossroads

At 5.30pm the main body of the Munsters was at the crossroads west of Oisy but without Captain George Simms and B Company. Charrier sent runners and cyclists out to find them but it was nearly an hour before they appeared, an hour of inactivity which was to prove fatal. Moving through Oisy, Captain Rawlinson's C Company brought up the rear of the battalion and almost immediately came under attack from General Karl von Plettenberg's *2nd Guard Division,* from which it was only just able to escape thanks to the covering fire from the two platoons of Lieutenant Deane Drake and Sergeant Foley. But now the consequence of the delay caused by B Company was beginning to manifest itself; further east the German advance was continuing as planned: General von Barfeldt's *19th Reserve Infantry Division* was heading towards Guise when the heavy firing to the north sent his reconnaissance patrols scurrying towards Fesmy. With signs of battle evident everywhere and rifle and artillery fire continuing through the afternoon, Barfeldt swung his division towards Étreux. The door was closing fast and it would be the *19th Reserve Division* which finally slammed it shut.

Karl von Plettenberg commanded the German 2nd Guard Division.

The last stand at Étreux

Moving onto the Oisy-Landrecies road and covered by Lieutenant Chute's machine gun section, 2/Munsters approached Étreux only to see enemy infantry crossing the road ahead of them. Before Charrier had

Lieutenant Challoner Chute was killed commanding his machine gun section.

time to deploy his men, a heavy fire was opened up on them from the houses on the edge of the town and a field battery from the direction of Le Gard. Almost before the 118/Battery guns were unlimbered one was destroyed with a direct hit; the other was hastily prepared for action but, having already fired over 300 rounds, ammunition was in very short supply and the number of gunners left alive or unwounded was diminishing fast. Undeterred, Charrier moved forward to discover that the enemy had occupied positions created by their own countrymen – trenches dug that morning by 1/Black Watch and a house which 23/Field Company had loopholed just off the road on the right. It was a twist of irony that would not have been lost on Major Paul Charrier; an irony which would prove to be the final straw in a rearguard action destined to catapult his battalion into British military legend.

Dividing into two, the battalion attacked to the left and right of the road. Struggling to bring the remaining gun to bear on the loopholed house, the gunners, including Major Bayly, who was wounded, were shot down in a hail of fire that came from both sides of the road even before the breech could be opened. Charrier led three charges against the loopholed house, Captain Douglas Wise, the battalion adjutant, actually getting close enough to fire his revolver through a window, only – according to the regimental history – to fall, stunned by falling masonry. It was now 7.00pm and the end was very near. Although held up by the loopholed house on the right, the attack on the left of the main road initially made progress. Lieutenant Erasmus Gower was with A Company:

> *Ordered to push on half went* [and] *pushed on* [the] *left of the road (East) other half on right – I went to* [the] *left. We pushed on through some orchards and a brickfield to a sunken lane near Étreux railway station – held up there. Captains Hall, Barratt, Lieutenants Sullivan, Crozier and self, supported by* [our] *fire, a charge* [made by] *Jervis' company. Only Jervis and three men got to the hedge, where* [they were] *taken prisoner.*

They had been stopped by the infantry of *Infantry Regiment 78* (IR 78) who had occupied the station and were firing from the cover of the railway embankment. But still the Irishmen fought on, refusing to give in to a force that by now completely surrounded and outgunned them. In

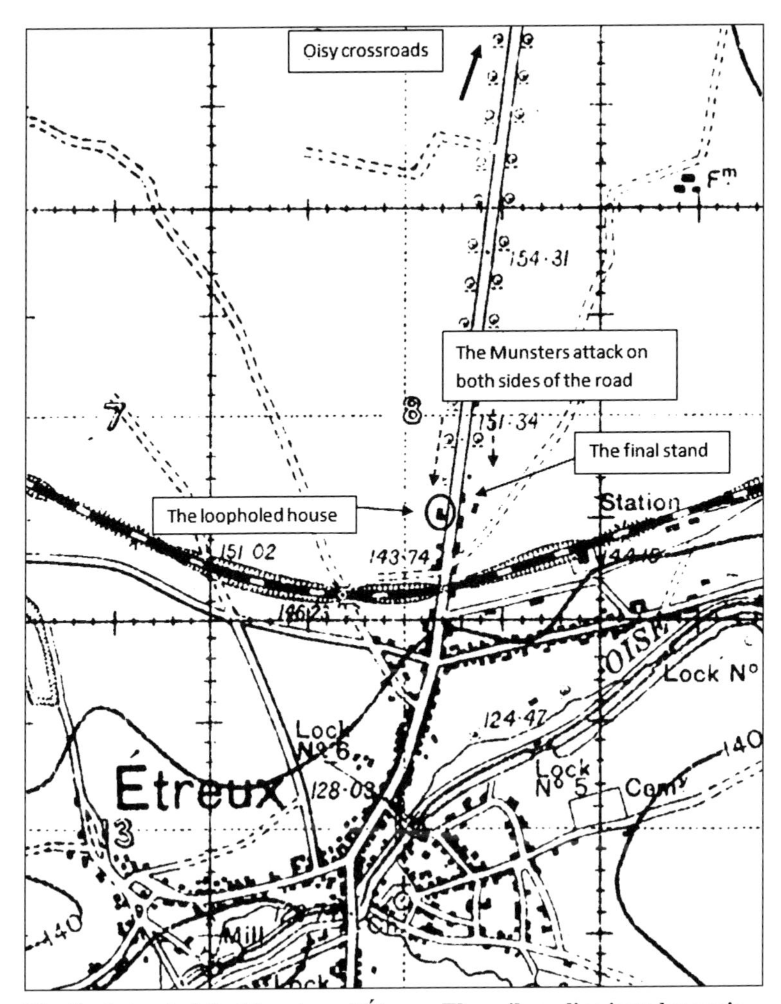

The final stand of the Munsters at Étreux. The railway line is no longer in use but other features, such as the loopholed house, still remain.

the final act of the day, in the gathering dusk, Captain Charles Hall and some 200 of the Munsters fell back to a small orchard near the main road – but not before they had lost Captain Phillip Barrett and Second Lieutenant James Crozier. Gower's account again:

> *When we got to the orchard I went to report to Major Charrier. I found him by the gun* [which was] *deserted as all the team of men were killed or wounded. Charrier* [was] *killed almost while* [I was] *talking to him, Rawlinson wounded at the same time.*

Lieutenant Frederick Styles was killed, along with six other officers and 112 NCOs and men.

Lieutenant Harry Newsome was taken prisoner at Étreux. He is seen here photographed at Torgau POW Camp.

C Company Royal Munster Fusiliers seen shortly before mobilization. Many of the men in this photograph would have fought at Étreux.

Returning to the orchard, Gower passed Captain George Simms lying dead and reported the death of Charrier to Captain Hall. In his absence, 20 year old Second Lieutenant Phillip Sullivan had been mortally wounded and young Challoner Chute killed next to his remaining machine gun. A last desperate bayonet charge to push the enemy out of the nearby lane resulted in Hall being badly wounded and command falling to Lieutenant Gower. It appears from Gower's account that the remaining men on the right side of the road attempted to break through at around 8.00 pm but were unsuccessful. Lining the four sides of the orchard, Gower's dwindling band of Munsters continued to keep the enemy at bay until it became obvious that further resistance was pointless. Gower then took what is probably one of the hardest decisions a soldier has to make:

> *Fresh enemy coming up from* [the] *north so surrendered at 9.12 pm – very little ammunition left ... I could hear no other firing to show any relief coming and was only losing men and doing no good. Also, fresh machine guns* [were] *getting into position. I surrendered with three officers and 256 men.*

They had been fighting for nearly twelve hours against a considerable force of von Bülow's *X Corps* in a rearguard action that enabled the main body of I Corps to put twelve miles between it and its pursuers.

Casualties

The battalion had landed in France with 1,008 officers and men and only 201 were present at a roll call on 29 August 1914. Nine officers and 112 men were killed, six officers and some 130 men wounded with four

The memorial cross erected soon after the battle to mark the grave of the fallen officers of the 2nd Munsters.

officers and over 400 men taken prisoner. Of 118/Battery RFA, seven men were killed, ten officers and men wounded and twenty-one taken prisoner. A fairly large body of men evaded capture and went into hiding in the local area. Exactly how many is unclear but estimates suggest that between fifty and 120 Munsters were still on the run a week after the battle. Some of these were able to get away with the help of escape organizations, such as those planned by Edith Cavell; whilst others were harboured by locals, many of whom were eventually captured in places like Iron, a few kilometres to the south, and shot by the Germans.

The retreat continues

When I Corps crossed the river at Guise there appears to have been some uncertainty as to whether the bridges were to be destroyed or left intact. The 23rd and 26th Field Companies prepared several bridges for demolition but in the event none was actually destroyed. Arrangements had been made to destroy the two bridges over the Sambre at Oisy after the Coldstream Guards had crossed but at the last minute these orders were cancelled by General Maxse. At Étreux Major Harry Prichard, commanding 26/Field Company, had been told to prepare the bridges over the Oise but his report that there were actually five – all within three quarters of a mile of each other – resulted in an order not to destroy them, presumably from General Maxse. What impact these demolitions might have had on the fate of the Munsters is impossible to say but the destruction of the road and rail bridges at Le Gard may have temporarily held up the *19th Division* as might the demolition of the road bridge over the Oise at Petit Cambrésis have delayed *X Corps*.

Despite the rearguard action at Étreux, the fighting continued for the remainder of Maxse's brigade all the way down the straight length of the road from Étreux to La Maison Rouge until well after dark. What was correctly assumed to be dismounted cavalry and German horse artillery was kept largely at bay by the four remaining batteries from XXVI Brigade, which came into action at Jerusalem Farm and La Maison Rouge. In his report to 1st Division Headquarters, Maxse drew attention to the brisk rearguard action that was executed with steadiness by the three arms in cooperation during the retirement and recommended seven officers for special mention. Lieutenant Charles Hardinge was included in the list but not one of the others was a Royal Munster Fusilier.

The repeated disappearing act which GHQ managed to sustain over the course of the retreat did little to enable it to recover control of the army and the confidence of the two corps commanders. GHQ continued to view events through hazy panes of gloom and doom, an atmosphere which must only have been intensified on 27 August with the loss of the

Munsters at Étreux . In a directive sent out that evening – which clearly illustrated GHQ's failure to recognize the tactical realities facing the BEF and did little to bolster the morale of the retreating troops – Henry Wilson ordered all unnecessary baggage and ammunition to be abandoned in order that exhausted troops could be carried on the transports.

Without doubt the physical state of the troops of II Corps after fighting two major engagements was very different to that exhibited by their counterparts of I Corps. Those who were in a position to draw comparisons thought that 'officers and men of II Corps were dirty and unshaven; units were a scratch lot with infantrymen on the wagons and limbers and stragglers all over the place'. Yet despite this poorly presented exterior, there were few signs of 'grousing and despondency'. The contrast between the two corps was quite marked; observers near Mont d'Origny early on the morning of 28 August noted the 'excellent appearance' of the British 1st Division. The men were tired and suffering from the extreme heat but marched in perfect order. Understandably, some of II Corps' regiments 'looked harassed ... there was some disorder and some units were intermingled'. GHQ staff officers had also returned reports of the poor state of II Corps, which may have contributed to the rather startling instruction issued by Henry Wilson to the Chief Royal Engineer Officer to reconnoitre and report on the

The pursuit of Haig's I Corps by the Second German Army was relentless. German infantry are seen here marching through a French town on their way to the Marne.

bridges that would have to be destroyed if the BEF retreated to La Rochelle – 250 miles southwest of Paris! It took a visit from Lord Kitchener on 1 September to steady the nerves of a panic-stricken GHQ.

The Battle of Guise

28 August was also a day that was remembered at the French Fifth Army HQ at Marle. Still with Lanrezac's staff as liaison officer, Lieutenant Spears recalled how 'a large figure which took up the entire breadth of the balcony' suddenly appeared. It was General Joffre himself. This was his first visit to Fifth Army Headquarters and one that Charles Lanrezac would have cause to bring to mind for some time afterwards. In the subsequent interview between the two men, Joffre apparently exploded with anger at his subordinate's reluctance to engage the enemy and made it clear that unless Lanrezac counter attacked immediately the Fifth Army would have a new commander. 'Joffre's Olympian anger bore fruit', observed Spears:

Joffre's Olympian anger encouraged Charles Lanrezac to turn and fight at Guise.

> *Lanrezac pulled himself together, and on that day at least a wave of energy vibrated down the nerves of the Army such as it had not known since it marched into Belgium.*

The thirteen columns of the French Fifth Army had been marching south on a front of about eighteen miles, this body of troops was now ordered to about turn and face northwest along a much narrower front. It was, to put it mildly, a Herculean task but one that was achieved just in time for the attack to begin at dawn on 29 August. In the hope that Haig would assist him, Lanrezac sent Captain Jacques Helbronner to test the waters of cooperation. Haig was found near Mont d'Origny and to Lanrezac's obvious delight expressed his willingness to support the Fifth Army. Haig's only reservation was that his participation in the attack should be agreed by GHQ. Spears was very apprehensive about this, 'I hoped and prayed that Sir Douglas's views would prevail with Sir John but felt terribly uncertain'.

Spear's apprehension was not unfounded; Sir John French refused point blank to cooperate and used as his justification the poor state of his troops – a further indication of the misapprehension that prevailed at the altogether too distant GHQ. I Corps was perfectly placed and well able to assist Lanrezac. With the French turning to face the German *Second*

French infantry at Guise turned the tables on von Bülow's Second Army and delivered their own 'Le Cateau' on 29 August.

Army at Guise, it appeared that Sir John was now getting his own back by rather petulantly refusing to support the French. Spears was horrified. The animosity created between the two army commanders at their first meeting at Rethel had come home to roost. For the first time since the war began the young lieutenant felt the British were in the wrong. The Battle of Guise was a resounding French success as Lanrezac's troops delivered their own 'Le Cateau' and temporarily stopped von Bülow in his tracks before turning to continue their retirement.

The Rearguard Action at Cerizy – 28 August 1914

By 28 August the distance between Smith-Dorrien and Haig had increased 15 miles and, for the first time since Le Cateau, two columns of German cavalry found the gap between the two corps south of St Quentin. The only British cavalry formations available to cover the gap were Brigadier General Hubert Gough's 3 Brigade in the west and Brigadier General Phillip Chetwode's 5 Cavalry Brigade in the east, who were providing the left flank guard for I Corps. The progress of the most westerly of the German cavalry columns was successfully scuppered by 4/Hussars and the guns of E Battery RHA. The eastern column – led by *2nd Guard Dragoons* – put up more of a fight. Moving down the main St Quentin-La Fère road – the N44 towards the

Brigadier General Phillip Chetwode commanded the 5th Cavalry Brigade during the retreat.

German Guard Dragoons

The Chateau at Mo   photographed before the outbreak of war. It was totally destroyed in 1917.

hamlet of La Guinguette – they occupied La Folie Farm. Less than a mile further south, Major Foster Swetenham and C Squadron of the Scots Greys were holding the wood north of La Guinguette, with the remaining squadrons of the Greys concealed amongst the undulating folds in the ground south of the D342 – the Moÿ-La Guinguette road. The 20/Hussars were on the high ground near Cerizy and in reserve were 12/Lancers, which were at the nearby twelfth century château at Moÿ.

Launching their attack just after 2.00pm against what they assumed was weak enemy infantry, a strong German force of two squadrons of the *2nd Guard Dragoons* galloped straight down the slope towards Swetenham's position in the woods at La Guinguette with the clear intention of testing the strength of the British positions. The combined fire power of J Battery's guns and the Scots Greys brought the charge to a disorganized standstill and those that were not killed or wounded bravely dismounted and returned fire.

Hearing shots from their château base at Moÿ, the 12/Lancers immediately saddled up and joined the Greys in directing fire onto the German cavalrymen who were still on the forward slope of the hill. With the arrival of two further squadrons of Lancers on the enemy eastern flank a dismounted firing line was quickly established. The next move was provided by the Lancers. Lieutenant Colonel Frank Wormald directed C Squadron to mount up and charge up the slope towards Puisieux Farm. Lieutenant Harold Charrington later recalled the moment the squadron topped the rise:

Lieutenant Colonel Frank Wormold.

> *With a ringing cheer, the squadron charged in perfect line across the fifty yards which now separated them from the enemy, with the Commanding Officer, his Adjutant, the Trumpet Major and two orderlies some twenty yards in front of them.*

Captain John Michell was killed almost immediately his horse went over the ridge, Trumpet Major Tompkins was badly wounded in the thigh and one of Wormald's orderlies was killed, the other unhorsed. The German position, wrote Harold Charrington, was completely overrun, 'hardly a man escaped, over 70 killed and wounded being counted on the ground afterwards'. Whilst most of the Germans rose to their feet to fight it out, they instinctively knew a bloody encounter was about to take place, as dismounted men caught in this manner by charging cavalry armed with swords and lances held no advantage. 'Our lances did great work,' wrote

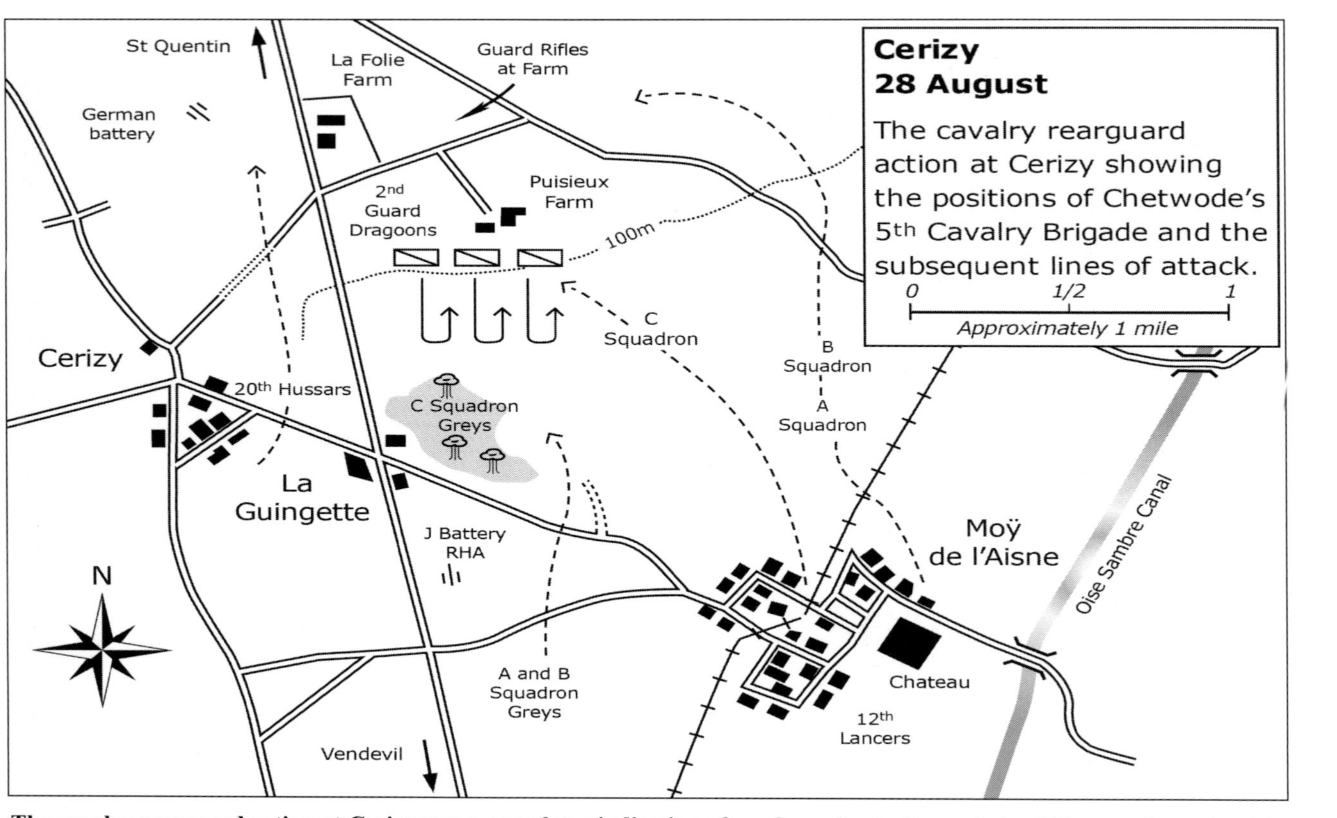

The cavalry rearguard action at Cerizy was a complete vindication of good cavalry tactics and should be seen in contrast to the disastrous encounter at Audregnies on 24 August.

An artist's impression of the cavalry charge by C Squadron, 12th Lancers.

Second Lieutenant John Leche, 'though they didn't go in as far as one would think – about a foot in most cases.'

As Michell went down at the head of the squadron, Colonel Wormald, using one of the new pattern Wilkinson thrusting swords, was dismayed to see it 'buckle like an S' as it skewered an unfortunate German. Lieutenant Charles Bryant had retained the old cutting sword and, well sharpened, it accounted for at least five of the enemy, 'going in and out like a pat of butter'. As soon as the squadron had ridden through the German position they were rallied by Lieutenant the Hon Richard Wyndham-Quin and charged back through the carnage of dead and dying before being rallied for the last time to dispose of any of the enemy who still had enough fight in them to stand firm. There were none. Indeed, by the time the two squadrons of the Greys arrived on the scene, the 12/Lancers had done their job so thoroughly that only unwounded prisoners were left to round up.

The 1913 Pattern cavalry thrusting sword.

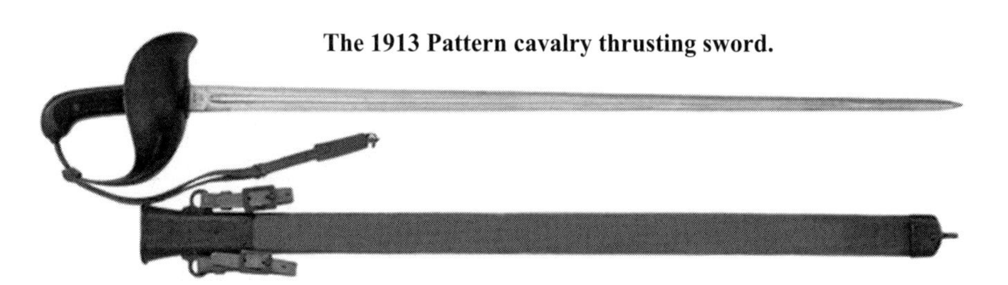

In the meantime, B and C Squadrons of 20/Hussars had been sent up the St Quentin road in a bid to get round the western flank of the enemy. As they breasted the rise they came under fire from two guns of the German horse artillery. Lieutenant Colonel Graham Edwards immediately decided to attack the guns; fortunately a charge was out of the question as numerous wire fences were seen in the vicinity. In response, the three troops of Captain Cecil Mangles' C Squadron dismounted some 200 yards from the enemy guns and began to put down heavy fire onto the German battery, an action which appeared to have the desired effect, as much of the battery's fire was then turned upon Mangles and his men who had, at least, achieved their aim of distracting the attentions of the German gunners from the main attack to the east. Lieutenant Sparrow's troop, which had been directed by Colonel Edwards to cover the right flank, took the opportunity to join in with the main attack and, wrote John Darling the 20/Hussars historian, 'had the satisfaction of getting home with their swords against some dismounted Germans', as did the regiment's French interpreter 'Chirby' Landier, who 'achieved the ambition of every Frenchman by killing a Bosche'.

A 1914 cavalryman.

J Battery Royal Horse Artillery were armed with six 13-pounder artillery pieces.

As 12/Lancers crested the ridge at the charge, J Battery concentrated its fire on whatever might be behind the dismounted German cavalry. Number 1 Section joined the two guns of 3 Section and together the four 13-pounders lengthened their range to sweep the hollows and copses to the north with shrapnel – fire which 'proved to be very effective against formed general troops ... throwing them into confusion'. The general troops referred to in the battery war diary were in fact infantry of the *Guard Rifles* who were assembling in a wood near La Folie, presumably in preparation for a counter attack – which, had it gone ahead, might very well have put a different slant on the day. Chetwode, in recognizing the potential seriousness of this threat, later acknowledged J Battery's accurate and timely fire on the *Guard Rifles* in front of the whole 5 Cavalry Brigade at Autreville, without which, he said, 'things might have gone badly for the brigade'.

29 August

The morning of 29 August saw the BEF halted in its overnight positions on the Oise. We know the French Fifth Army was attacking towards St Quentin in the opening moves of the Battle of Guise but for the BEF – apart from the cavalry units involved in the fighting along the Crozat Canal and the Somme – the day was devoted to rest and repair. Behind the scenes there was considerable unease as to the intentions of the BEF. Joffre visited Sir John French at Compiègne to ensure the BEF remained in line with the French on both flanks and continued the retreat in line with the French Fifth and Sixth Armies. Joffre was right to be concerned, as Sir John wanted to withdraw the BEF and allow it to refit and recuperate – a notion that surely indicated his lack of awareness as to the strategic situation facing him. It was not until 9.00pm on 29 August that he issued orders for the retreat to continue behind the Aisne.

Stage 3

Villers-Cotterêts to the Marne

In this section we look in detail at the action of 4 Guards Brigade in the Forêt de Retz, north of Villers-Cotterêts. We begin at Soucy and follow their retirement to the crossroads west of Puiseux-en-Retz and then to the forest road that runs through the Rond de la Reine. Here you will find the evocative Guards' Grave Cemetery and the magnificent Cecil Memorial, lasting reminders of the fight in the forest. From Villers-Cotterêts we then briefly follow the I Corps retreat through Boursonne and Betz before concluding at the Marne, where I Corps crossed the river at Trilport and Meaux on 3 September.

Background

The first day of September 1914 was one of those days on which the pursuing German forces may very well have dealt a serious blow to the BEF's ability to continue the fight had events dictated a different outcome. On 30 August the gap between Haig's I Corps and Smith Dorrien's II Corps finally closed and a day later, on 31 August 1914, III Corps came into being under the command of Major General William Pulteney. This comprising the 4th Division and the independent 19 Infantry Brigade, which was later temporarily absorbed into the 6th Division after the latter landed in France on 10 September. Marching west, Pulteney's Corps moved down the western bank of the Oise and reached the neighbourhood of Verberie late that night. Haig and I Corps crossed the Aisne at Soissons, with 5 and 23/Field Companies blowing the bridges behind them.

III Corps was formed on 31 August under the command of Major General William Pulteney.

On 31 August II Corps halted for the night southwest of Villers-Cotterêts at Croyolles and at Crépy-en-Valois. I Corps halted for the night on the northern edge of the Forêt de Retz, the 1st Division around Missy-aux-Bois and the 2nd Division around Laversine. The astute observer with one eye on the map will quickly recognize that there were quite considerable gaps between the infantry divisions of the BEF, gaps through which large bodies of German forces could pass unnoticed. The source of the problem lay almost entirely with GHQ's Operational Order Number 12, which failed to establish the boundaries for which each formation was to be responsible and left it up to each corps commander to decide how much of the area allocated to them would be used.

The rearguard action at Villers-Cotterêts - 1 September

The action in the forest north of Villers-Cotterêts was the third of the major attacks made on the BEF on 1 September. Early that morning I Corps was converging on Villers-Cotterêts through the Forêt de Retz; while the 2nd Division's route took it through Vivières to the Rond de la Reine, a small forest clearing some three miles north of Villers-Cotterêts. 4 Guards Brigade was ordered to provide the rearguard for the 2nd Division.

The previous day 2/Grenadier Guards had been on the road since 7.15am, marching in the blazing heat for most of the day before they

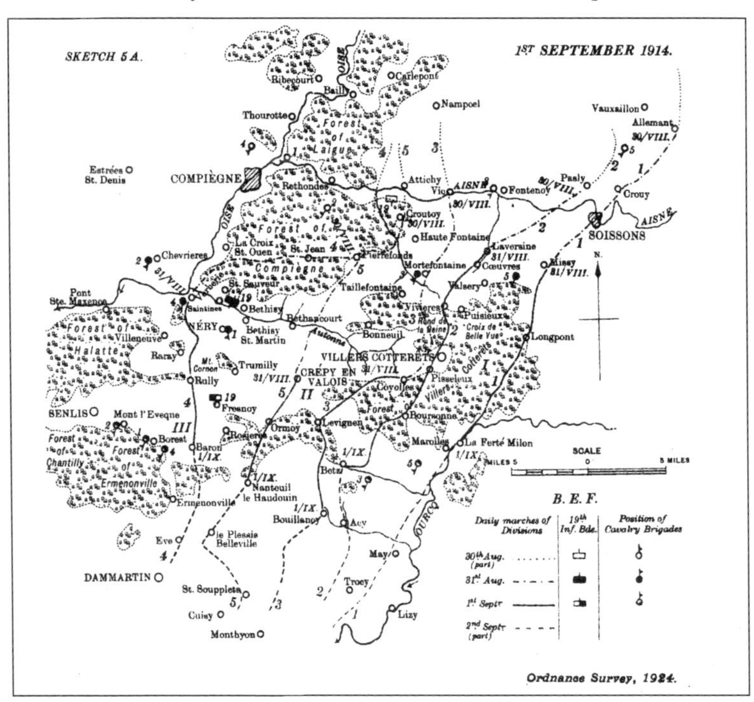

A map taken from the Official History 1914, Volume 1, depicting the lines of retirement taken by each division of the BEF south of Carlepont.

finally bivouacked just north of Soucy. But the heat – although debilitating – was not foremost on the mind of Major Bernard Gordon Lennox. His diary gives a hint of the general feeling of frustration experienced by many of the officers of 2/Grenadier Guards on what was the eighth day of the retreat: 'We now know that as soon as a gun is heard – be it five miles off or twenty-five miles – we shall be shortly inundated with orders to march, to be followed shortly with counter orders.' It was not as if it was all the fault of the brigade staff. Gerry Ruthven, the brigade major, complained on several occasions that he was given no information at all regarding the disposition of enemy troops – or for that matter where other British units were either. Lieutenant Colonel the Hon George Morris, commanding the 1st Battalion Irish Guards (1/Irish Guards), was uncharacteristically pessimistic in his assessment of the situation, reckoning that it was the old problem of allies falling out with each other and predicting that the BEF would be embarking for England within a fortnight.

Morris was correct on one count; if the retreat was beginning to nibble at the morale of the men it was also putting a dent in Anglo-French relations. On 29 August Joffre drove to Compiègne to plead with Sir John French not to withdraw from the line altogether; French's reply was not what Joffre wanted to hear. The BEF, declared Sir John, was on its last legs and desperately needed rest and recuperation. His opinion was unchanged on 31 August, when Sir John told Kitchener in no uncertain terms that the BEF could do little until it was re-equipped. It would take another highly charged meeting between Kitchener – in his role as Secretary of State for War – and Sir John at the British Embassy in Paris on 1 September to settle the nerves of the British Commander-in Chief. If Sir John felt he would be able to withdraw the BEF and refit with the intention of re-joining the conflict at a later date he had badly misjudged the nature of what was taking place. The BEF was committed whether he liked it or not and his five divisions were fighting for their very existence.

Lieutenant Colonel George Morris, 1/Irish Guards.

I Corps was underway by 4.00am on 1 September. At Soucy the orders for the day woke the commanding officers of the four Guards' battalions a little after midnight and as soon as it got light orders were issued to dig in and hold their positions to cover the retirement of the 2nd

Division. Major Jeffreys, with the 2/Grenadier Guards, recalled the moment the orders arrived:

> *The CO was deadbeat, and was sleeping like a log when orders came in soon after midnight. I shook him but he couldn't wake up properly, and when I said 'Orders' he said 'you deal with them' and slept again. The orders were to take up and entrench a rearguard position on the line Mont Gobert-Soucy spur north of Viviers: Grenadiers to be on the right, 3rd Bn. Coldstream on the left. The 5th and 6th Brigades were to pass through us.*

Field Marshall Horatio Herbert Kitchener

The morning opened with a thick mist and the passage of British units was almost spectral as they moved slowly south towards the leafy cover of the forest. Lieutenant Aubrey Herbert – ever poetic in his diary account – thought the movement of 5 and 6 Infantry Brigades was like 'the sound of deep, slow rivers passing'; the more practical Bernard Gordon Lennox thought their hilltop position would become a regular shell trap once the mist dispersed.

First contact

Shortly after 6.00am the mist had lifted a little and right on cue probing German cavalry patrols began to appear – only to be driven off by rifle

Led by Lieutenant Colonel Noel Corry, the 2nd Battalion Grenadier Guards marches out of Le Havre on 15 August 1914.

fire. Nevertheless, Bernard Gordon Lennox's judgment of his battalion's position soon proved to be correct when a German battery opened up on them at 6.30am, fortunately coinciding with orders to fall back onto the Rond de la Reine. As the Grenadiers retired through 1/Irish Guards and 2/Coldstream – both battalions under the overall command of George Morris – Bernard Gordon Lennox took a few minutes to chat with an old friend and former Grenadier Guards officer, Major Hubert Crichton, who was now second-in-command of the Irish battalion:

> *He asked me what was going on. I told him nothing special, only the usual strategic movement to the rear. Half an hour later he was dead, poor lad, and the brigade and the world are the losers.*

The Irish Guards had deployed on the high ground just north of Puiseux-en-Retz. The first appearance of German troops advancing towards the village prompted Colonel Morris to send Aubrey Herbert with a message for Lieutenant Colonel Cecil Pereira, commanding 2/Coldstream, who were lining the edge of the forest to his left. It was an eventful ride:

> *I went off at a gallop, and had got halfway there, with the wood on my left and open land on my right, when the Germans began shooting at about three-quarters of a mile. Our men were firing at them from the wood, and I felt annoyed at being between two fires and the only thing visible to amuse our men and the Germans.*

As he made the return journey to the Irish lines it was becoming evident that both battalions were coming under heavy attack from a large body of troops on what appeared to be a wide front. Four miles further west, 3 Cavalry Brigade was already engaged with the advanced guard of the German *III Corps* and had been since 9.00am. At Taillefontaine, on the north western edge of the forest, Lieutenant Colonel Ian Hogg's 4/Hussars were under attack from cavalry and infantry advancing out of Roye St Nicholas, the small village to the north that Colonel Hogg's men had vacated only a few hours earlier. With orders to hold a line in the forest until 12.30pm, A and C Squadrons were gradually pushed back by sheer weight of numbers, during which the 39 year old Colonel Hogg was seriously wounded while directing C Squadron's retirement. Ian Hogg, the son of the well-known educational philanthropist, Quintin Hogg, died of his wounds the next day in the schoolhouse at Haramont.

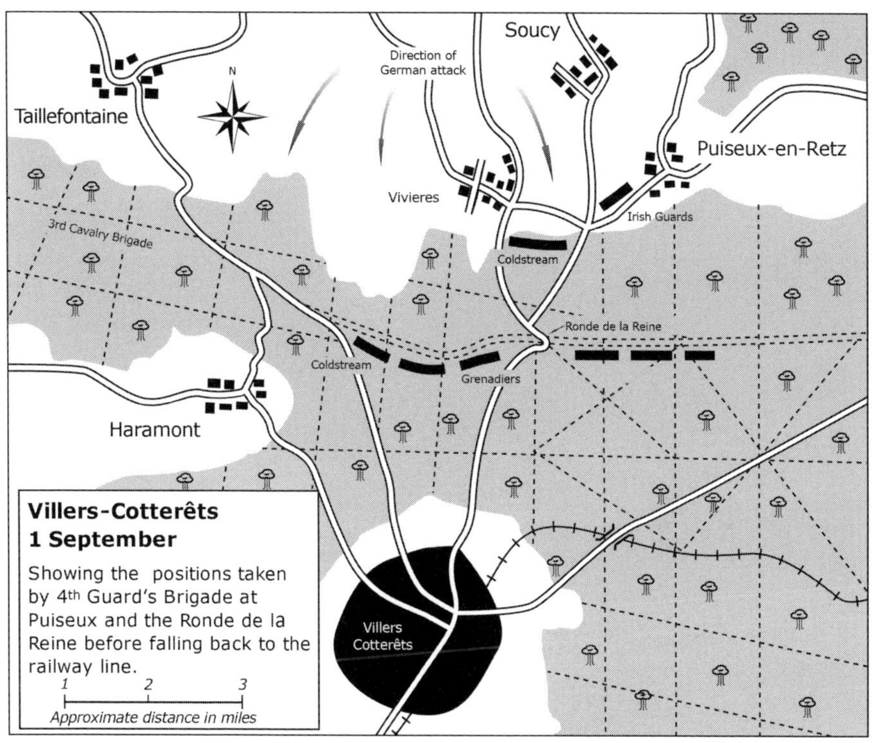

Although under pressure, the 4 Guards Brigade fought a classic – but costly – rearguard action in the forest north of Villers-Cotterêts.

The retirement from Puiseux

In the meantime the two battalions of Coldstream and Irish Guards were holding their own at Puiseux and with the help of 9/Battery RFA were effectively bringing the German advance to a halt. Suspecting that the enemy had been temporarily discouraged from further offensive action, Morris sent word again to Colonel Pereira with instructions for his battalion of Coldstream Guards to fall back to the railway line north of Villers-Cotterêts. Morris was preparing to follow them when he was taken aback by a rather surprising order from brigade ordering him to stay put, as the main body of the division was to halt for their lunches until 1.00pm. The Coldstream were already past recall by this time, which left the Irish Guards isolated and extremely vulnerable; in Aubrey Herbert's considered opinion, if the division took too long over their lunches the Irish Guards would probably be wiped out – a view shared by Major Jeffreys on the Ronde de la Reine with the Grenadiers.

The 1st Battalion Irish Guards outside Wellington Barracks, prior to leaving for France.

Jeffreys' astonishment at the order was only tempered by the arrival of some of Chetwode's 5 Cavalry Brigade, who halted at the Rond de la Reine and dismounted:

> *We all had a good many friends amongst the officers, we stood talking together for quite a considerable time, a risky proceeding considering how vulnerable their horses were, and that they were masking our fire should the Germans come on. As it was it was very pleasant coffee-housing in the shady ride for all the world like a big field hunting in the New Forest on a spring day.*

The respite at the Ronde de la Reine proved to be only temporary and was soon shattered by the sounds of heavy firing to the north as the Irish Guards came under attack again. Aubrey Herbert described the Germans advancing towards their front and on the left flank at about 10.45am. 'There was a tremendous fire. The leaves, branches, etc, rained upon one. One's face was constantly fanned by the wind from their bullets.' Attacked on all sides, the Irish had no choice but to fight a very costly running battle through the woods, with the Germans almost on top of them. Aubrey Herbert was acting as the commanding officer's galloper and consequently remained close to George Morris during the fight. He described the retirement of the Irish Guards back to the Rond de la Reine:

Men were now falling fast. I happened to see one man drop with a bayonet in his hand a few yards off, and reined in my horse to see if I could help him, but the CO called me and I followed him. The man whom I had seen was Hubert [Major Hubert Crichton], *though I did not know it at the time. The CO ... had a charmed life. He raced from one place to another through the wood; cheering the men and chaffing them, and talking to me; smoking cigarette after cigarette.*

The Irish Guards retire

The Irish Guards were falling back on the line running west-east along the two rides that centred on the Rond de la Reine and where the Grenadiers had established their battalion HQ. Lieutenant Colonel Noel Corry, commanding the battalion, had placed Numbers 1 and 2 Companies on the rising ground about 100 yards south of the main ride east of the Rond de la Reine and Number 4 Company along the ride to the west, where they were in touch with 3/Coldstream Guards. The Coldstream were widely extended along the ride in an effort to block the enemy from using the numerous rides which ran from north to south. Altogether it was not a good spot for a fight, particulalry with the dense undergrowth making communications difficult and fields of fire almost impossible.

Company by company, the Irish Guards fell back onto the Ronde la Reine, pursued by what Bernard Gordon Lennox described as 'the green Jaeger fellows'. At some point in their retirement Colonel Morris was killed, becoming the first commanding officer of the Irish Guards to fall in battle. His death was a huge loss to a battalion that had also just lost its second in command. A man noted for his bravery and composure under fire, not half an hour before his death, after a period of sustained shellfire which brought trees crashing down, he had called to the men: 'D'you hear that? They're doing that to frighten you.' To which

The Irish Guards' Machine Gun Section.

someone replied, 'If that's what they're after, they might as well stop. They succeeded with *me* hours ago.'

It was not long before the gaps on the left of the line were being exploited and fighting became a confused mêlée as German forces attempted to get round the left flank. Major Jeffreys:

> *The first I heard of what was happening on my left was when Gerry Ruthven appeared leading a horse on which was the Brigadier, badly wounded and obviously in great pain. He shouted to me that the enemy was held but we should shortly have to withdraw, and disappeared to the rear in the Forest.*

With Brigadier General Scott-Kerr wounded, command of the brigade fell to the Grenadiers' commanding officer, Noel Corry. But taking over command of a brigade in these circumstances was well nigh impossible and in truth no one was effectively in overall command as the three battalions of Guards began to fall back to the bridge over the railway line north of Villers-Cotterêts – not an easy move by any means. The Coldstream companies and Irish Guards to the west of the Rond de la Reine were forced to fall back diagonally behind the Grenadiers – a manoeuvre they carried out with characteristic parade ground discipline as they withdrew behind the Grenadiers under a hail of fire. Bernard Gordon Lennox's company on the right of the line gave covering fire before they too began filtering back towards the railway:

> *The firing on my left was very hot and the opposing forces were in some cases only 70 yards off each other ...* [then] *the companies on my left were ordered off to the left to reinforce and I also sent one platoon along. Everyone was now mixed up hopelessly and officers just took command of whatever men they found. We now got the order to retire slowly on Villers-Cotterêts.*

With Jeffreys now in command of the Grenadiers, the battalion eventually got over the railway bridge, having successfully navigated the maze of forest rides, owing their successful retirement to the cool and professional aura of command that Jeffreys possessed and the fact the Germans were having some difficulties navigating the criss-cross pattern of rides in the forest. Nevertheless, all three Guard's battalions took casualties before they finally shook off the advancing enemy. Jeffreys was left very much to his own devices:

Once over the bridge I assembled the battalion ... and we marched off down the road and through Villers-Cotterêts. We had no orders. The Brigade organization had, I suppose, been upset by the Brigade Major escorting the wounded Brigadier out of action. Our CO had gone off with what remained of Brigade Headquarters, so we just followed the rest of the brigade.

Casualties

The brigade had taken some 360 casualties, many of whom had been left wounded and dying in the forest glades as the Guards fell back to Villers-Cotterêts. Some would not be discovered until it was too late; others were more fortunate and fell into the hands of German ambulance units, where they received attention. One of these was Aubrey Herbert, who had been shot at close range with a bullet through his side. Managing to remain on his horse he made it back to an aid station:

I got off and asked them to take on my horse. Then I lay down on the ground and an RAMC man dressed me. The Red Cross men gave a loud whistle when they saw my wound, and said the bullet had gone through me. The fire was frightfully hot. The men who were helping me were crouching down, lying on the ground. While he was dressing me a horse – his, I suppose – was shot just behind us. I asked them to go, as they could do me no good and would only get killed or taken themselves.

One of the earliest photographs of the mass grave that later became the Guards Grave Cemetery

The Guards Grave Cemetery shortly after construction.

As the Guards retired through 6 Brigade, which had established a defensive line on the southern approaches to Villers-Cotterêts, two companies of 1/ Royal Berkshires – the same battalion which had fought at Maroilles a week earlier – were instrumental in holding off the German advance, which very nearly overwhelmed the six guns of 70/Battery. Rising to the occasion once more, the Royal Berks, with the help of a company of South Staffords, held off the enemy long enough for the gun teams to limber up and bring the guns out intact. This was no skirmish, the Royal Berks lost over twenty five NCOs and men;35 year old Captain Harold Birt, commanding C Company, was awarded the DSO for his part in the action. Birt was killed in January 1917 when a shell hit the C Company shelter in the trenches at Festubert.

Altogether the fighting south of the town left another 160 casualties. Eighty of the wounded had been picked up by Numbers 4 and 5/Field Ambulances whilst Number 4/Field Ambulance – many of whose men had already been taken prisoner at Landrecies – had established a dressing station in a nearby sugar factory. It was only the next morning, after the medics realised that they had been left behind, that they narrowly escaped the fate of their comrades at Landrecies.

The move over the Marne

The *Official History* tells us the Army was growing hardened to the retirement but personal accounts from the diaries of officers and men involved in the retreat tell a different story. Haig was certainly concerned about the large numbers of men who were falling out exhausted and unable to continue, so much so that on 1 September he ordered half the ammunition that was being carried by his divisional ammunition columns to be sent on by train, thereby releasing fifty wagons to carry kits and exhausted men. Haig's actions would have been loudly supported by Private Arthur Cook, whose diary account reflected the physical state of the majority of the BEF in early September:

> *We marched for 12 hours continuously and the heat and dust were cruel, almost unbearable. We are feeling the effects of all this marching, but our platoon officer, Lieutenant Pretyman is smiling. He found a stray horse and goes along in front of us stretched out on the horse's back, fast asleep. We expect to see him fall off any minute but he doesn't. Today's march was 28 miles over roads inches thick in dust. We look like a lot of millers, our clothes, faces and hands covered in dust, our mouths horribly parched. Everyone has a beard and with no washing facilities we look a set of horrors. Our numbers are gradually declining, with men falling out each day.*

On 2 September, I Corps was on the eastern right flank of the BEF retirement with II Corps on their left. 5 Cavalry Brigade covered the

British cavalry approaching the Marne crossings.

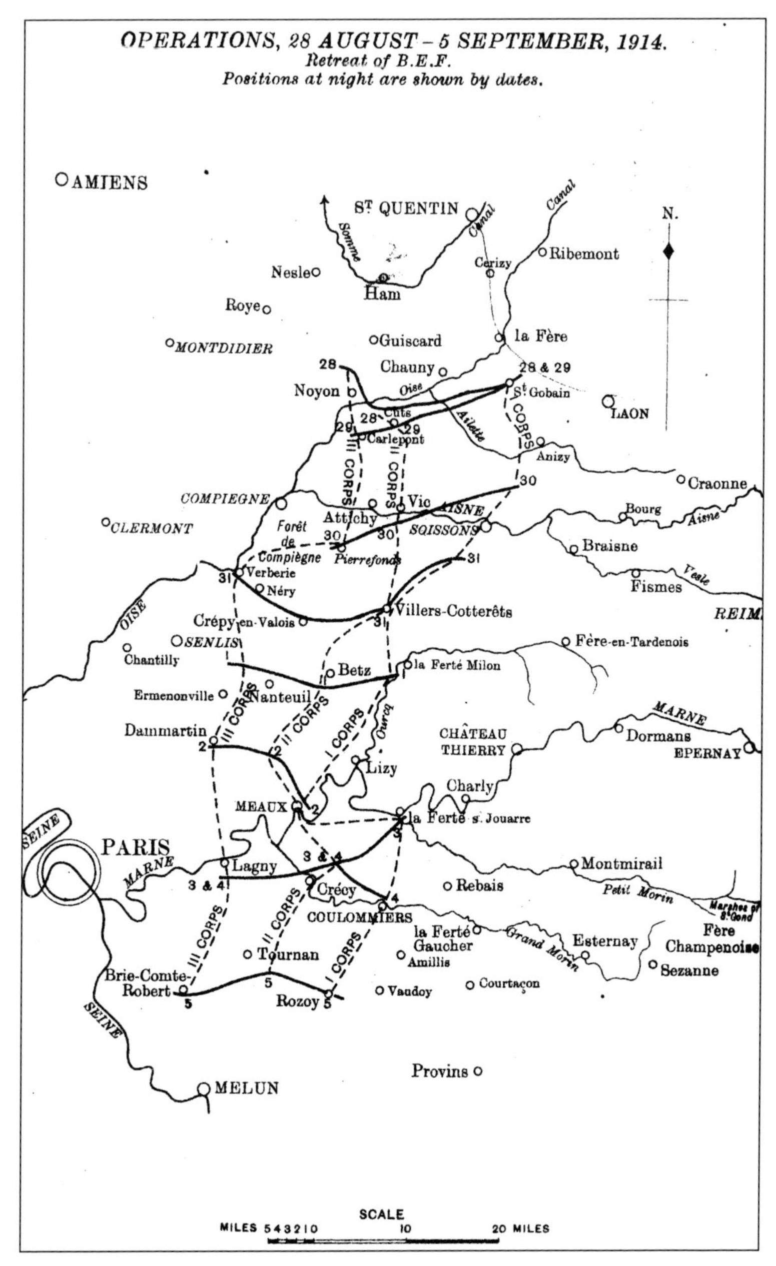

A map taken from the Official History 1914 Volume 1 of the lines of retreat taken south of St Quentin. Although the map depicts three separate lines, they should be seen as a guide to the routes taken by the main bodies of each corps. 4 Guards Brigade we know retired through Betz on their way to Meaux.

eastern flank of I Corps. With the Marne a little over twenty miles to the south, the BEF was largely untroubled by enemy interference. 4 Guards Brigade halted at Puisieux for breakfast and bivouacked that evening near Rolentier after a march through the heat of the day of twenty two miles.

Having started between 3.00am and 4.00am, the Marne was crossed by the 1st Division at Trilport on 3 September, closely followed by the 2nd Division at Meaux. The ever faithful 5 Cavalry Brigade, which encountered a short burst of enemy rifle and artillery fire at May-en-Multien, crossed the Marne at La Ferté-sous-Jouarre. Altogether it had been a trouble free crossing and at 11.50am Sir John French issued orders for the remaining Marne bridges to be destroyed and for the BEF to continue its retreat southwards. The retreat ended on 5 September; during the thirteen days that had elapsed since the Battle of Mons the Army had marched nearly 200 miles with an average of four hours' rest in every twenty four. The politics behind the GHQ Operational Order No 16, which in effect signalled the final day of the retreat and a largely unnecessary march, are outside the scope of this book but on the morning of 6 September the three army corps of the BEF turned northwards and began its slow ponderous move into the Battle of the Marne, taking their place between the French Sixth and Fifth Armies. The retreat was over.

Following Haig's Retreat

Maps

The route is best supported by the Belgian IGN 1:50,000 Series and the French IGN 1:100,000 maps, which can be purchased at most good tourist offices and online from www.mapsworldwide.com. However, I have used satellite navigation on numerous occasions and found it to be particularly helpful in supporting route finding. For iPad users, the Michelin maps of Belgium and France, which have a good search function and additional information on hotels and restaurants, are also highly recommended. For the walker and cyclist, the larger scale 1:20,000 or 1:25,000 Series maps can be bought in Belgium and France or, alternatively, online. I do recommend that you use the relevant large scale map segment when out walking or cycling.

Getting there

By far the quickest passage across the Channel is via the tunnel at Folkstone, the thirty five minutes travelling time and ease of disembarkment comparing favourably with the longer ferry journey from Dover. Whether your choice of route is over or under the Channel, early booking well in advance is always recommended if advantage is to be taken of the cheaper fares. Depending on where you are intending to base yourself and at which stage of the I Corps retreat you are joining the tour, the following approximate travel times may be useful:

Calais to Mons is two hours travelling using the A25 and the E42
Calais to Landrecies is two hours travelling using the A26
Calais to Cerizy is one hour fifty minutes using the A26
Calais to Villers-Cotterêts is two hours forty-five minutes using the A26 and A1

Driving abroad is not the expedition it was years ago and most battlefield visitors these days may well have already made the journey several times. However, if this is the first time you have ventured on French roads there are one or two common sense rules to take into consideration. Ensure your vehicle is properly insured and covered by suitable breakdown insurance; if in doubt contact your insurer, who will advise you. There are also a number of compulsory items to be carried by motorists that are required by French law. These include your driving licence and vehicle registration documents, a warning triangle, a *Conformité Européenne* (CE) approved fluorescent safety vest, headlamp beam convertors and the visible display of a GB plate. Whereas some modern cars have built in headlamp convertors and many have a GB plate incorporated into the rear number plate, French law also requires the vehicle to be equipped with a first aid kit, a fire extinguisher and, in order to comply with the law, it is a good idea to include a breath test kit. If you fail to have these available there are some hefty on the spot fines for these motoring offences if caught driving without them. Most, if not all, of these items can be purchased at the various outlets at the Tunnel and the channel port at Dover and on board the ferries themselves.

Driving on the 'wrong side of the road' can pose some challenges. Here are three tips that the author has always found useful:

1. When driving in France on single carriageway roads try to stop at petrol stations on the right hand side of the road. It is much more natural then to continue driving on the right hand side of the road after you leave. Leaving a garage or supermarket is often the time when you find yourself naturally turning onto the wrong side of the road.

2. Take your time! Don't rush! If you rush your instinct may take over and your instinct is geared to driving on the left.

3. Pay particular care on roundabouts. A lot of French drivers do not and appear rarely to use indicators. Navigators remember to look at the signs anti-clockwise and drivers remember that the danger is coming from the left.

On a more personal note it is always advisable to ensure your E111 Card is valid in addition to any personal accident insurance you may have and have a supply of any medication that you may be taking at the time.

It goes without saying that walkers and cyclists should come to Belgium and France properly equipped to enjoy their activity. The weather is often unpredictable and it is always advisable to walk in a decent pair of boots and carry a set of waterproofs with you.

Where to stay

Bearing in mind that the I Corps retreat from Mons does not seriously encounter German forces until Landrecies, I have confined any recommendations for accommodation to points south of Bavay. From experience I have found the Farm Ribeaufontaine at Dorengt near Étreux to be comfortable and well appointed. The farm caters for bed and breakfast only, but the accommodation is first class and you will be assured of a welcome and a superb breakfast. (http://ribeau fontaine.jimdo.com). Early booking is recommended. Campers will appreciate the all year round facilities at Camping Le Fromental at Gommegnies.

Moving further south from Étreux and Guise, Noyon can serve as a useful base. The town lies one hour south of Guise and boasts the magnificent cathedral of Notre-Dame de Noyon, where the first Holy Roman Emperor, Charlemagne, was crowned in 768. The town is less than an hour from Villers-Cotterêts. Just outside the town is the 2 Star Ibis Budget Hotel, which gives good value; but if you are looking a little more up-market, the 3 Star Hotel le Cèdre in the cathedral square offers a secure car park. Camping in the area is plentiful but I can recommend Camping La Montagne at Chirry-Ourscamp, which can be found approximately five kilometres south west of Noyon. The site is open all year round, has a pool and mobile homes for rent. Further south, at Château Thierry I have found the Campanile to offer a basic overnight stay with the added advantage of an on-site restaurant. Campsites in this area of the Marne abound, but I can recommend the 4 Star Camping at Village Parisien at Varreddes, near Meaux, which has all the facilities one would expect, including a large swimming pool.

With children in mind

This is not the ideal tour on which to include children and young people who have no or little interest in events that took place a century ago. However, the new museum at Mons should prove attractive to young and old alike. It is to be housed in La Machine à Eau, a 19th-century building that, until 1961, supplied Mons with its drinking water. The permanent collection will include much of the town's impressive archive from the First World War – uniforms, drums, medals, photographs, letters and more. The museum is due to open in time for the start of the city's year as European Capital of Culture in 2015.

Just east of Bavay at Feignies, is Fort Leveau, which was part of the Maubeuge fortifications of 1914. Here you will find reconstructed trench lines and a museum which again will hold some fascination for the young and is well worth a visit if you have the time. Bike rides are always popular with children and the countryside south of Noyon around the canals and forests abound with cycle trails. The tourist office at Noyon can supply maps and routes as can the tourist office at Villers-Cotterêts for the bike trails in the Forêt de Retz.

At Meaux the newly opened Museum of the Great War – *Musée de la Grande Guerre* – has something for everyone and the displays should engage all ages. The museum has a café and there is a large parking area where picnics are possible.

Unexploded ordnance

Regular visitors to the battlefields will be familiar with the collections of old shells and other explosive material, often placed at the roadside by farmers. This lethal harvest is less likely to be observed over the course of the retreat from Mons but there are still occasions when you may chance to come across unexploded devices of 1914-18 vintage or even ammunition remaining from World War II. The rule is quite simple – by all means look and take photographs but please do not touch.

Stage 1 Tour

Landrecies to Le Grand Fayt

This thirteen mile tour begins at Landrecies, where Douglas Haig's I Corps had its first taste of close quarter action with the enemy. The town can be approached from the west using the D643 from Cambrai or from the north on the D934 from Valenciennes.

Begin at the Sambre Canal bridge on the D934 **[1]** where you will find the memorial to **Lieutenant General Sir James Ronald Edmonstone Charles,** who commanded the 25th Division from August 1918 until the end of the war. The 25th Division liberated Landrecies on 4 November 1918. As you stand on the bridge with the memorial behind you, the Hachette Bridge to the north of Maroilles is to your right and Ors – where the poet **Wilfred Owen** is buried in the communal cemetery - is along the towpath to your left. It was this bridge that Rommel used to cross the Sambre in May 1940 with his 7th Panzer Division, an acute reminder of another painful period of French Military history.

When the alarm was raised at 8.00pm by the Coldstream picquet at Faubourg Soyeres, the bridge was immediately barricaded by No. 4 Company of 2/Grenadier Guards under the command of **Captain the Hon Edward Colston**. The streets ahead of you were plunged into chaos. Brigadier General John Charteris, who was military secretary to

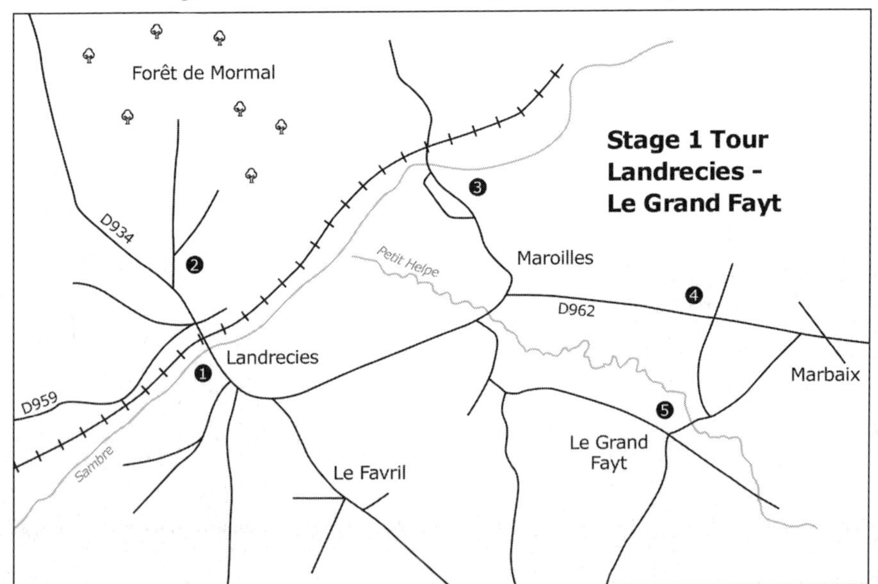

The memorial to Lieutenant General Sir James Ronald Edmonstone Charles.

The Sambre road bridge at Landrecies looking down towards the railway station. The bridge was barricaded by Number 4 Company, Grenadier Guards, on the night of 25 August.

The modern day railway station at Landrecies is on the same site as its 1914 predecessor.

The memorial tablet commemorating the Coldstream's action.

The memorial arch north of Faubourg Soyeres.

Sir Douglas Haig, recalled men throwing mattresses out of windows for the barricades, 'I saw one rather pompous and unpopular staff officer walking towards me, and a man in an upper window, taking deliberate aim with one of those great soft French mattresses, and hitting him fair and square with it'. Rejoin your vehicle and drive slowly towards the bridge over the railway, passing the recently restored former French military barracks on the right where Douglas Haig was billeted before he left the town shortly after the German attack began. Just before the bridge take the slip road on the right to pass under the bridge to the railway station. Park here. This is where **Major Bernard Gordon Lennox** and his No. 2 Company were deployed just after he and his company officers had sat down to enjoy their evening meal: 'We were in the middle of our dinners about 8.30pm when the alarm went off and we rushed out to hear heavy firing going on outside our end of the town. Everyone fell in hurriedly, there was a good deal of skurry but no disorder.' With the battalion at battle readiness, Nos. 2 and 3 Companies were ordered down to the level crossing to deploy left and right. Anticipating a German flanking movement around the Coldstream picquet at the Faubourg Soyeres, Major Gordon Lennox and his No. 2 Company doubled down to the station buildings where you are now, while No. 1 Company deployed in the streets just behind the station. Across the road was No. 3 Company covering the right flank. It was not long before German troops began infiltrating across the railway line. 'We waited quietly', wrote Major Gordon Lennox, 'and saw a couple of dull red glows, which were no doubt the lamps of the leading officers. We opened a salvo of rapid fire and one of the lights disappeared to be followed shortly afterwards by the other one.'

Using the one way system, retrace your steps and continue over the road bridge to a small roundabout and go straight across and up the hill. After passing through the private houses at Faubourg Soyeres you will see the memorial arch **[2]** to the Coldstream Guards on the left; park where convenient and walk across to the memorial. Here you will find a plaque dedicated to the Coldstream action. This is the approximate position of **Private Thomas Robson's** machine gun and where **Charlie Monck** and **Robert Whitbread** were standing when German forces first approached the Coldstream outpost. According to a map drawn by **Lieutenant the Hon Rupert Keppel,** the area directly behind the memorial arch is where much of the action took place. The Coldstream barricade was across the road immediately before the minor road on your left. ***Leutnant* John** and *Infantry Regiment 27* (IR 27) approached Landrecies along the D934, which you can see straight ahead of you, a road which was lined on either side in 1914 by tall poplar trees. On the left of the road, beyond the screen of trees, you can see behind the water reservoir a large white house which, in 1914, had a walled garden. As the attacking infantry of *IR 27* consolidated their positions, the south facing garden wall was loopholed and a trench was dug in the field to your left.

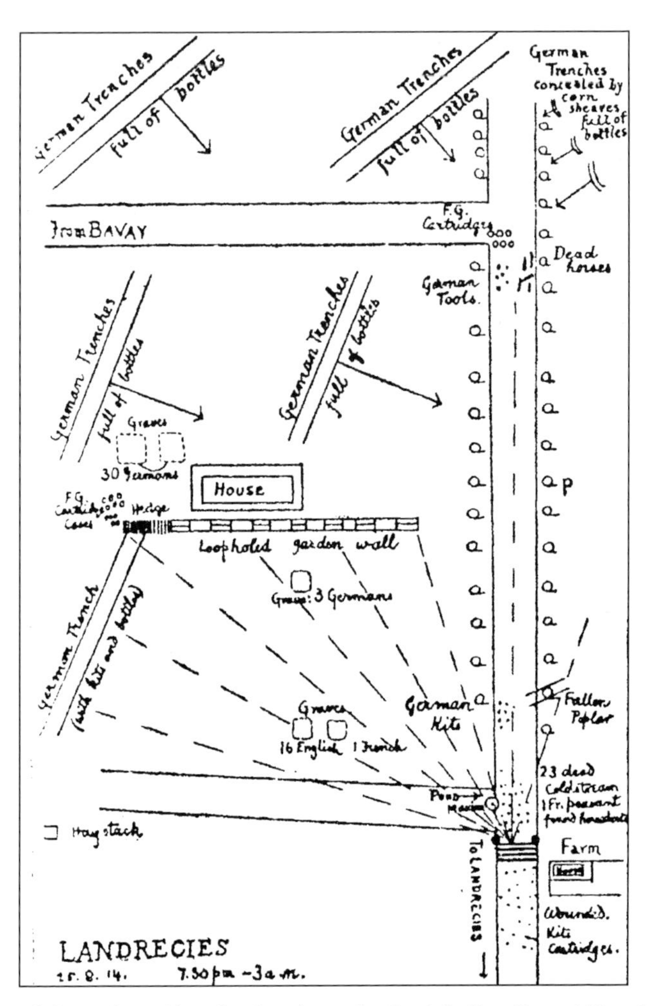

A map of the action at Landrecies drawn by Captain Hon Rupert Kepple, 3rd Battalion Coldstream Guards, after his capture.

Behind the house more trenches were dug, facing obliquely towards the road. Remember, by this time it was dark and raining heavily, the troops of both sides were wet through and tired, and while the enemy could be heard, only the muzzle flashes from their weapons could be seen in the darkness.

By 10.00pm the situation had become distinctly unpleasant; two of the German guns had been manhandled into position across the fields and were now firing on the Coldstream picquet and on the town itself and much of the town north of the canal was on fire. **Major the Hon Torquil**

Matheson was now in overall command of the Coldstream and led the defence for the next four hours, and, according to Private Paddy Smythe, 'put new heart into the men with his total disregard of personal danger'.

Sometime after this a haystack along the minor road to your left was set alight, presumably by shellfire, illuminating the Coldstream positions. This is where **Lance Corporal George Wyatt** reacted and ran out under fire on two separate occasions to extinguish the blazing stack. It was a very brave act from an individual who had been walking the beat as a Barnsley policeman before he was called up on 5 August. His subsequent Victoria Cross was presented by the King at Buckingham Palace in March 1916.

With German losses mounting and little progress being made against the Coldstream, *Infantry Regiment 165* (IR 165) was ordered up to assist *IR 27*. The Germans had little idea of the strength of the British units in front of them but it appears from their account that the darkness and difficult nature of the ground in front of them was enough to deter a determined advance. Further discouragement arrived soon after 1.00am in the form of at least one British gun, which had been brought up from the level crossing and which, 'fired point blank at the flashes of the German field guns and had the effect of silencing them'. This effectively brought the action to an end as German accounts tell us their own guns were withdrawn and the two regiments of infantry dug in to the left and right of the main Englefontaine road. By 3.00am on 26 August the leading columns of 4 Brigade were continuing their retreat towards Étreux . The encounter with the German *7th Division* had robbed them of any chance of snatching much needed sleep and ahead lay yet another long day on the road.

Return to your vehicle and drive back down the hill towards Landrecies. We are now going to travel east to Maroilles, which is ten minutes away along the D962. As you re-cross the Sambre road bridge and drive through Landrecies, keep a sharp look out for the communal cemetery on your left.

Landrecies Communal Cemetery

This is a large communal cemetery. Go through the main gate next to the chapel and look out for the distinctive CWGC Cross of Sacrifice across to your left. The British and Commonwealth plot contains fifty three identified Commonwealth graves from both World Wars, the majority of which can be found in the War Graves Plot. There are also eight isolated plots scattered around the cemetery. There are twenty four 1914 burials here, nearly all resulting from the attack on the town. The German dead are commemorated by a large memorial dedicated to the *gefallenen*. **Private Thomas Robson**, the machine gunner who was bayoneted at his post, lies in B.6., surrounded by some of the men who defended the road north of Faubourg Soyères so tenaciously. The majority of the other ranks are buried in a communal grave. Three notable officers are

The CWGC plot at Landrecies Communal Cemetery.

amongst the dead; 23 year old **Lieutenant the Hon Archer Windsor-Clive** and **Lieutenant Sir Robert Cornwallis Maude** were both serving with 3/Coldstream Guards and **Second Lieutenant Robert Vereker** serving with 2/Grenadier Guards. Robert Vereker was a cousin of Lord Gort VC, the BEF Commander-in-Chief in 1940, and had only been in the battalion for eleven months. 24 year old Robert Cornwallis was commissioned in 1912 and also held the titles of 6th Viscount Hawarden and the Baron de Montalt. He died of shrapnel wounds early on the morning of 27 August.

There are seven RAF aircrew buried in rows B and C, all casualties from May 1940. 19 year old **Leading Aircraftman (LAC) Frederick Bettany** was part of a two man crew flying a 26 Squadron Lysander when he was shot down and killed. His pilot, **Flying Officer Ralph Clifford,** lies in Neuvilly Communal Cemetery Extension near Le Cateau. 18 May 1940 was a black day for 15 Squadron, three of their Blenheim IVs were shot down whilst attacking German motorised columns at Le Cateau and a fourth crashed on landing after the raid. **Flight Lieutenant Paul Chapman** and his crew of **Sergeant Cecil Colbourn** and **LAC Ernest Fagg** died in Blenheim P6917 and **Flying Officer Francis Dawson-Jones**, **Sergeant William Baxter** and **LAC Cyril Watts** died in Blenheim L8852.

Maroilles

From the cemetery continue along the D959 towards Maroilles from where the D32 will take you north to the Hachette Bridge **[3],** which crosses over the Sambre. Drive over the bridge to the railway station and

The Hachette Bridge, north of Maroilles.

park; ahead of you is the vast Forêt de Mormal. You will find a small restaurant here which is usually open for coffee and snacks. You are now on the German side of the action that took place here on the night of 25 August. The Hussars were initially deployed between the railway line and the bridge before they were driven back over the bridge. It was on this side of the river that Major Turner was taken after he was captured.

A view of the railway station at Hachette. German forces approached the bridge from the Forêt de Mormal, which you can see in the distance.

After returning to your vehicle drive back over the bridge to take the first turning on the right and park. This is a narrow road and is the beginning of the original causeway that led into Maroilles until the D32 extension was built. It was along this causeway that German troops advanced until they met the men of the 1/Royal Berkshires. Walk up towards the bridge to where there is a sloping track on the left down to the river bank. The Berkshires advanced up towards the bridge and deployed along the river banks from where **Henry Shott** swam the river.

Return to your vehicle and continue along the causeway to join the D32 at a T-junction with a large information board on the right. Turn right

The causeway along which the Royal Berkshires approached the bridge.

and continue towards Maroilles, turning left at the junction to pass the bandstand and village green on your right. The communal cemetery is straight ahead of you. Parking is available by the entrance.

Maroilles Communal Cemetery

Here you will find eighteen of the Berkshires buried together in a communal grave, which is why most of the headstones bear the names of two men. There is also a private memorial to 37 year old **Henry Hammond Shott,** erected by his American wife Hazel; and a much larger ornate memorial that appears to have been provided by the local community. In 1896 Henry Shott joined Colonel Plumer's Matabeleland Relief Force as a trooper and served throughout the Matabele War, remaining in Africa until 1897. He enlisted in Bethune's Mounted Infantry in November 1899 and was commissioned in 1900. His award of the DSO in recognition of his services in South Africa came a year later in 1902 - as did his transfer to the Royal Berkshire Regiment. In 1913 he gained his Royal Aero Club Certificate, flying a Bristol Biplane at Brooklands.

Maroilles Communal Cemetery and the gr of the Royal Berkshires killed at the bridg

Le Grand Fayt

From Maroilles Communal Cemetery return to the main road and turn left to the D962 and drive east towards Marbaix for approximately a mile, passing over two minor sets of crossroads, until you reach the Taisnières-en-Thiérache crossroads **[4].** To the left is the narrow road leading to Taisnières-en-Thiérache and to the right is the minor road to Le Grand Fayt. Take the turning on the right to Le Grand Fayt and stop where convenient. Walk back to the crossroads where B Company and the remaining men of C and D Companies had been left after **Colonel Abercrombie** marched off towards Marbaix. The men would have been in the surrounding fields.

Ahead of you the road to Taisnières-en-Thiérache is marked by the distinctive water tower in the distance. Before long the crossroads became the focus of German horse artillery shell fire announcing the forthcoming arrival of German units from the *10th Reserve Jäger Battalion* (10/RJB). Consider yourself for a moment in the place of **Major Alexander,** commanding the remainder of the battalion at the crossroads. The commanding officer has vanished in the direction of the enemy and left no orders regarding your next move, you are under fire and expecting the arrival of German cavalry and motorised infantry. Placing your men on alert and ordering outposts to be positioned, you decide to remain where you are until 6.00pm, at which point you move downhill into Le Grand Fayt. There you find blazing buildings and retiring French territorial troops, all of which convinces you to begin marching towards Étreux. Alexander's decision to march south certainly prevented an even greater disaster befalling the battalion.

Return to your vehicle and move down the road towards Le Grand Fayt, passing the bulbous shape of the meterological station on your left.

The Mairie at Le Grand Fayt. Brigadier General Herman Landon would have had his HQ here and Douglas Haig would have undoubtedly made this his first port of call after leaving Landrecies on 25 August.

The Mill at Le Grand Fayt. It would have been close to this building that Colonel Abercrombie and the Connaughts were ambushed.

You will soon see a farm on the right next to a plantation of trees. Stop briefly where convenient. Look across to the left where you should be able to get an impression of the difficult nature of the country facing Colonel Abercrombie and his party as they retired downhill towards Le Grand Fayt. Across to your left and somewhere near this road was where Abercrombie deployed a small rearguard commanded by **Captain Francis Leader**. With him was **Lieutenant Gordon Barker's** machine-gun section and **Second Lieutenant Charles Turner** with a platoon from D Company. Abercrombie had only just moved off towards the village when the rearguard party came under heavy attack.

Just after dusk, outgunned and enfiladed, Captain Leader was killed and Barker fired the last round from the one remaining machine gun and took charge of the few men that remained. Ordering them to fix bayonets, he led them in a last counter attack during which he was brought down by a bullet in the thigh and Charles Turner was hit twice in the shoulder, leaving him dazed and only partly conscious. The British survivors spent the night in the field and were taken the next morning in a cart to Avesnes-sur-Helpe, though the German account suggests they were first taken to Marbaix.

Continue downhill towards the village, joining the D117 just before you cross the river. It is likely that this is the route by which Abercrombie and his small part of men entered the village sometime after 7.00pm **[5]**, passing the mill on the left. Told by an inhabitant that there were no German forces in the village, the Rangers were ambushed minutes later by a strong force of Germans hidden on either side of the road. Pandemonium prevailed as officers and men scattered in all directions; some, as we know, succeeded in eventually rejoining the battalion but Colonel Abercrombie and his party were later captured at Maroilles.

Le Grand Fayt Communal Cemetery

The cemetery can be found on the D232 to Petit Fayt and marks the conclusion of the Stage 1 Tour. The main British and Commonwealth plot is in the south eastern corner of the cemetery, where there are five identified casualties. At the rear of the plot stands an imposing memorial cross erected by the Germans commemorating the British, German and French soldiers killed at Le Grand Fayt on 26 August 1914. On either side is a headstone, each one recording the deaths of three unknown Connaught Rangers. In the centre, at the foot of the cross, is a flat headstone commemorating nine unidentified British soldiers and seven – 3 unidentified - German soldiers of *3 Company, 10/RJB*. What is interesting about this German memorial is that the seven casualties whose names appear on the headstone – and are referred to in the regimental history - were never reinterred and their names do not appear in the *Volksbund* database of German casualties. This must be one of

The British and German graves at Le Grand Fayt Communal Cemetery.

the very rare cases of German casualties remaining in their original tomb in a French communal cemetery.

Amongst the identified British casualties is 33 year old **Captain Francis Leader,** who served with the embodied militia in the South African War before he was commissioned into the Connaught Rangers in 1903. His promotion to captain came days before he left for France in 1914. Buried with him are **Lance Corporal Edward McCann,** who enlisted in 1912 and 23 years old **Lance Corporal John Wyley**. Both men were probably killed with Captain Leader during the rearguard action north of the village. Another Connaught, Private Michael Molloy, who was one of the wounded moved to Avesnes-sur-Helpe, later died of his wounds on 4 September and is buried in Avesnes Communal Cemetery. Both the 1918 burials are against the wall on the immediate left of the entrance and are casualties of the 'advance to victory'. **Captain Robert Clark** was the medical officer attached to the 20/Hussars and died of wounds three days before the Armistice. On 6 November 1918 the Hussars were at Le Grand Fayt and held up by German machine gunners just north of the river at Le Pas de Laliau. Captain Clarke was hit attending the wounded. 26 year old **Major Edward Chisholm** of the Canadian Field Artillery and the holder of the Military Cross and two bars was commanding C Battery, 161 Brigade. Chisholm was one of the youngest battery commanders in the CFA and was killed nearby by machine gun fire on the same day as Robert Clark.

Stage 2 Tour

Chapeau Rouge Crossroads to Cerizy

This tour covers forty two miles of the retreat. Our first stop is at the Chapeau Rouge crossroads **[1]**, where the D934 from Landrecies is intersected by the D643/D1045. Park in the restaurant car park and walk across the road to the 1st Division Memorial. Take care here, as the crossroads can be busy. This rather splendid memorial was designed and sculpted by Richard Reginald Goulden in 1926 and inaugurated in the presence of Lieutenant General Sir Arthur Holland, Marshal Foch and Sir Peter Strickland, who commanded the division from 1916 until the end of the war. In August 1977 the memorial was moved by the 32nd Engineer Regiment to its

The 1st Division Memorial at the Chapeau Rouge crossroads.

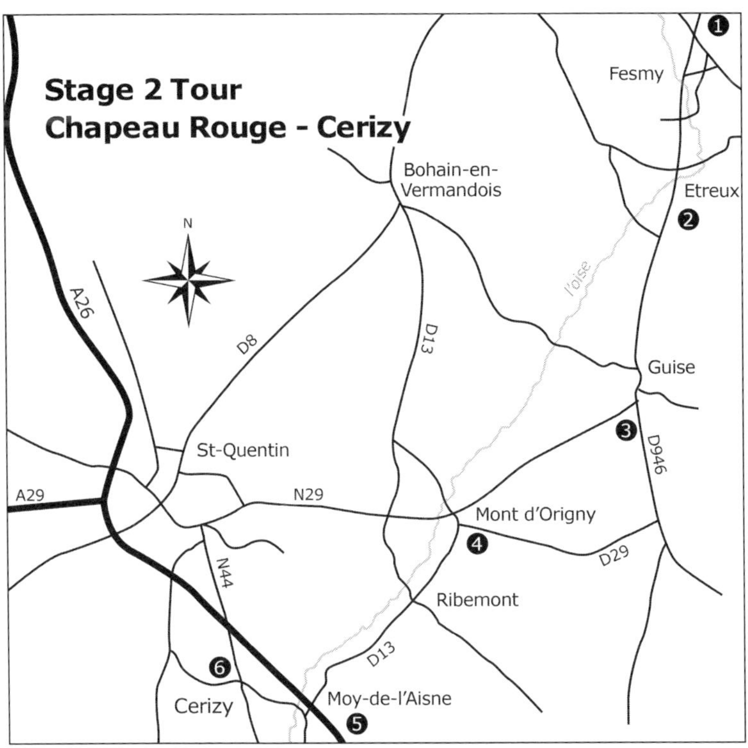

present position after being hit several times by passing traffic and was restored and rededicated.

From the memorial look back up the road to the north and La Groise. Just beyond the last building on the left D Company straddled the road into the fields on the right. Now walk back across the restaurant car park and look up the road towards the industrial buildings you can see across to your left. In the far distance is the church tower of the Nativité de la Sainte Vierge at Cattilon-sur-Sambre. Between the car park and the industrial buildings **Captain George Simms** and B Company formed an arc across the road into the fields on the left, forming a protective screen against German forces approaching from the north west. There was fierce fighting here as both companies were engaged by the enemy advance patrols.

At around 1.00pm, in torrents of rain and under severe pressure from an increasingly tenacious enemy, both companies slowly withdrew, B Company down the road towards Oisy and Étreux and D Company along the D634 towards Fesmy-le-Sart. As D Company retired the two guns of 118/Battery came into action just north of the D66 crossroads.

Fesmy-le-Sart

Return to your vehicle and take the D643/D1043, signposted Bergues-sur-Sambre and Boué in the direction of Fesmy-le-Sart. This is the road along which D Company retired from the crossroads as they made their way to Fesmy. Take the first turning on the right – D66 - into Fesmy-le-Sart village and park near the church. It was along this minor road that one platoon from A Company under **Lieutenant Erasmus Gower** escorted the guns of 118/ Battery guns into the village.

The Church at Fesmy-le-Sart.

Major Paul Charrier had his headquarters near to the church and would have been delighted to have seen D Company arrive along with the 118/Battery guns and Lieutenant Gower. But there was little time for niceties, hot on their heels were the first units of German infantry, who managed to penetrate the village before they were expelled by C Company. The Munsters' retirement to the Oisy crossroads followed the D663, which you will find running south from the church. At the junction with the D663 pause and look across to the left, towards Bergues-sur-Sambre, where A Company were rescued by the 15/Hussars. Charrier himself may well have stopped here to refer to his map and perhaps even to consult with **Major Bayly** before the remaining Munsters crossed the Sambre just east of Oisy and waited at the crossroads for B Company to arrive.

The crossing point over the Sambre at Oisy, which the Munsters would have used on their way to the Oisy crossroads.

Étreux

Turn left at the Oisy crossroads and continue towards Étreux **[2].** Just before the road crosses the former railway line you will see Étreux British cemetery on the left. Park here. It was near to this spot that Charrier gave orders for the battalion to attack on both sides of the road. Look across to the house with the metal gates which lies at right angles to the road on the opposite side. This is the 'loopholed house'. Ironically, the building had been prepared for defence by 23/Field Company that

Étreux British Cemetery.

The loopholed house. The present day building is probably much the same as it was a hundred years ago.

very morning but now the Germans were taking full advantage of it, along with trenches dug earlier by men of 1/Black Watch. The irony would not have been lost on a character like Paul Charrier. The German defence of the cottage would prove to be the final straw in a rearguard action destined to secure a place for his battalion in British military legend.

Now walk downhill towards the spire of Étreux church and take the first turning left along the lane which bears left past a large calvary. The lane soon becomes a farm track, which can be very muddy in wet weather. You are now walking parallel to the main road and soon the rear of Étreux British Cemetery comes into view across a field to the left. Although Paul Charrier was held up at the loop-holed cottage opposite the cemetery, the attack on the left hand side of the main road initially made progress in spite of several men being killed or wounded. **Captain George Simms** led the charge of A Company across country, parallel to the main road and towards the orchard - now the site of the cemetery - but was cut down as he reached it. To his left, Boer war veteran **Captain Herbert Swynfen Jervis**, in command of D Company, had extended the Munsters' line to the east. In spite of the losses, officers and men ran on through the orchard and across the field to your left in a series of short rushes as far as this lane. **Lieutenant Erasmus Gower** was with A Company and had been ordered to push forward to the left of the main road towards the railway station. Up ahead and to the right you will be able to see a line of willow trees running out across the fields towards what looks like a hedge line. This line is the top of what was the railway embankment. With A Company giving covering fire, **Captain Jervis** urged D Company on across the field to your right towards the railway

The former railway station at Étreux is now a private dwelling and home to an assortment of motor vehicles.

embankment, in the direction of the distinctive transmitter mast, in an attempt to break the German line and create a gap through which the Munsters could escape. Lieutenant Gower watched as the Munsters were shot down by *Infantry Regiment 78,* (IR 78), leaving only Jervis and three of his men to be taken prisoner. Now walk back to the cemetery, which was the scene of the battalion's last stand and where Lieutenant Gower finally surrendered his men late that evening.

Étreux British Cemetery

In March 1921 the family of Lieutenant Frederick Styles bought the orchard at Étreux from the owner, a **Monsieur Charles Dauzet**, for the sum of 500 Francs. The ground was consecrated seven months later by the Dean of Wassigny on 5 October 1921. Amongst those who attended the ceremony were the parents of **Lieutenant Vere Awdry**, **Captain Richard Chute** - the brother of the battalion's machine gun officer – and Frederick Styles' two brothers and sister. The cemetery is now under the care of the CWGC.

As you enter the cemetery a magnificent Celtic cross stands flanked by two rows of headstones placed along the south and north boundary walls and arranged in alphabetical order. At the rear of the cemetery are the two mass graves where the dead were buried after the battle, while along the rear wall four further headstones are flanked by two stone crosses – on the left commemorating the officers and on the right the NCOs and men. Above the central stone bench is a plaque explaining what took place here on 27 August 1914. There is only one unknown soldier buried here and his headstone lies next to **Private William Wilkes** by the rear wall. Nine of the 2/Munster's officers are buried here. **Second**

The plaque at the rear of the British Cemetery at Étreux explaining what took place on 27 August.

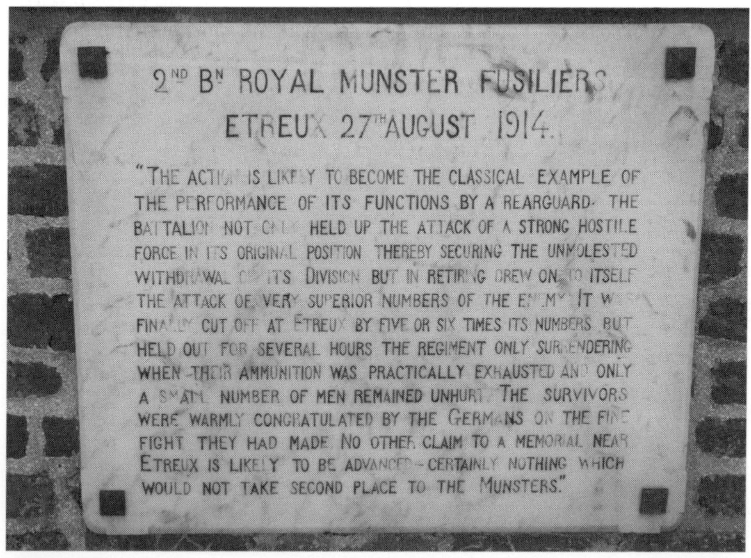

Lieutenants Vere Awdry (II.3.), who had been a foundation scholar at Marlborough before being commissioned, **James Crozier** (II.2.), who studied medicine for two years before joining the battalion in June 1914 and **Phillip Sulivan** (II.1.), who joined the battalion in February 1914 and whose epitaph simply reads, *'Died on his 20th birthday'*. You will also find the gallant **Lieutenant Challoner Chute** (II.6.) and **Charles Phayre** (II.5.), whose grandfather was General Sir Robert Phayre. Tragically, his brother, Lieutenant Richard Phayre, was killed later in the year at Ypres whilst serving with the 2/Yorkshire Regiment. Close by is **Frederick Styles** (II.4.), the special reservist who was recalled on the outbreak of war and **Captains Phillip Barrett** (II.7) and **George Simms** (II.8.), who are next to their commanding officer, 45 years old **Major Paul Charrier**.

Guise and the Fifth Army Memorial

Just after passing through the historic town of Guise **[3]** you will come to the junction with the D946, where you will find the large Fifth Army Memorial commemorating the Battle of Guise, which was fought on 29 August. Many I Corps' units would have passed this very spot having marched through Guise. There is ample parking behind the monument. Should you wish to visit the French National Cemetery at Flavigny-le-Petit, continue along the D946 for a mile and a half.

The Fifth Army Monument at Guise.

French National Cemetery at Flavigny-le-Petit (La Desolation)

The cemetery contains the graves of French and German soldiers killed during the Battle of Guise and during the 1918 offensives, together with a number of French colonial troops killed during the May 1940 fighting. The cemetery was begun by the Germans in 1914 and enlarged again after the Armistice. In the centre is a tall German monument in grey

The German memorial at Flavigny-le-Petit.

The British graves at Flavigny-le-Petit.

stone; on either side and behind the monument are buried 2,332 German soldiers, of which 911 are in an ossuary. There is also a row of Belgian troops. In front of the monument are two mass graves containing 2,643 French soldiers, of whom 1,493 are in two ossuaries. The forty seven British graves – including five unknowns - are all from the 1918 fighting, apart from 20 year old **Private William Barham** of 3/Coldstream Guards, who died of wounds on 26 August 1914.

From the cemetery continue to Mont d'Origny **[4]** via the D29 and take the D76 to Origny-Ste-Benoît. At the junction with the D29 you should pick up signs for the German Cemetery at Origny-Ste-Benoît. There are 3,942 German graves here and, before they were moved to St Souplet British Cemetery, the cemetery also contained twenty three British graves from the period March/April 1918. Less than half a mile away along the minor road to Pleine-Selve is a tiny French cemetery consisting of a mass grave containing eighty seven casualties of the Battle of Guise. To find it return to the junction and take the road that runs past the water tower.

After leaving the cemetery you can either continue to Pleine-Selve and take the D58/D13 via Ribemont or retrace your steps to Origny-Ste-Benoît and follow the D131 south. Either way your destination is Moÿ de l'Aisne, a short journey of some twenty five minutes.

Moÿ de l'Aisne and Cerizy

Drive into the town **[5]** and park by the church opposite the Gendamerie. You are now quite close to the site of the former château. If you look across the road with the church on your left, towards the industrial buildings, the ground beyond the trees is where the château once stood; sadly this magnificent building was completely destroyed in 1917. The château is where the 12/Lancers were billeted on 28 August when they heard firing from near La Guinguette farm.

The view from the N44 of La Guinguette Woods and Puisieux Farm.

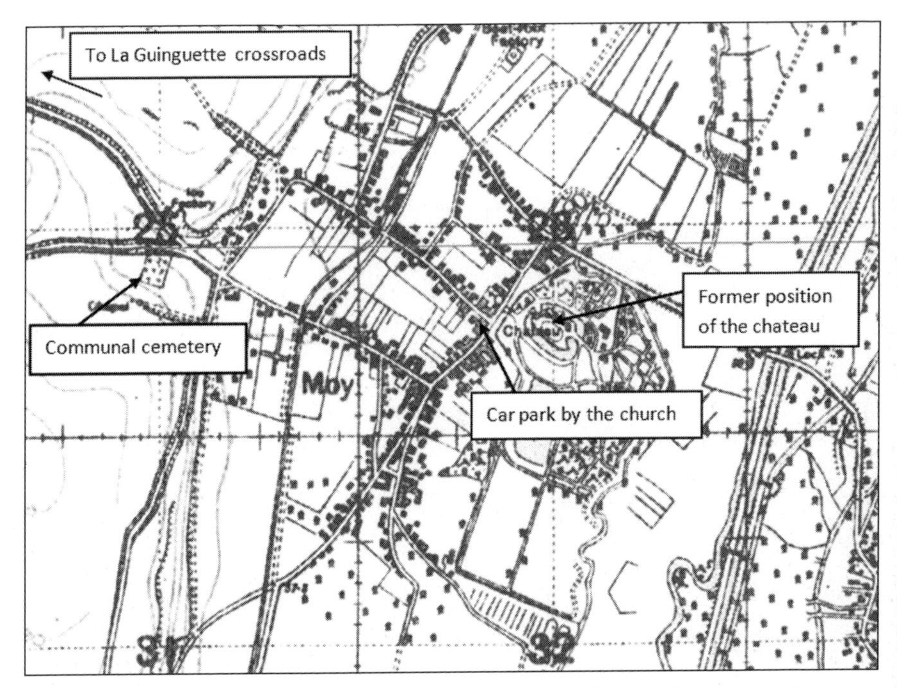

Moÿ as it was in 1914 showing the location of the former chateau and the position of the car park by the church. Note the present day communal cemetery has remained on the same site.

Take the D342 out of the town to the La Guinguette crossroads **[6]** and turn right towards St Quentin. After 300 yards you will see a layby on the right where you can park your vehicle. Take the track leading from the layby towards the copse you can see ahead of you on the right. This is La Guinguette Wood, where **Major Foster Swetenham** and C Squadron of the Scots Greys were positioned. Swetenham was killed in this vicinity as he directed the fire of his squadron. Walk along to the wood, where you will get an excellent view of the slope down which the German *Guard Dragoons* charged towards the Greys. The wood ahead of you in the distance is Bois Frémont. The shallow valley in which you are standing is the Vallée de Hôtellerie and the farm that you can see on the high ground to the north is Puisieux Farm. The former site of La Folie Farm is further across to the left, nearer to the road. The high ground you can see to the left of the main N44 is where the 20/Hussars were positioned, just north of Cerizy village. The J Battery guns would have been positioned on the ground around the crossroads.

If you look across to the right you should be able to make out the A26 Motorway and it was from this direction that the 12/Lancers attack came after they left the château at Moÿ. They dismounted in the dead ground near the motorway and brought a heavy fire down on the already retiring *Guard Dragoons*. The Lancers charge, by C Squadron led by **Captain**

Puisieux Farm.

John Mitchell, took them to the top of the rise to the left of Puisieux Farm and it was there that Mitchell died at the head of his squadron.

Puisieux Farm

Return to your vehicle and drive up the hill for half a mile to the obvious junction, taking the right turn along the narrow metalled road towards Puisieux Farm and stop where convenient. Walk back to the junction and look across the road to the high ground on the other side; it was from the direction of Cerizy that C Squadron of the 20/Hussars arrived to attack the German guns. If you look to your right, La Folie Farm once stood approximately where the large electricity pylon stands today. Return to your vehicle and either walk or drive along the track past the turning to Puisieux Farm to where the track meets the motorway, bearing left to the small bridge. From this point you can perhaps appreciate the lie of the ground across the fields towards La Guinguette Wood and get some idea of the nature of ground over which the 12/Lancers approached the German cavalry. I suggest you now return to the communal cemetery, where some of the casualties of this action are buried.

The CWGC plot at Moÿ Communal Cemetery.

Moÿ Communal Cemetery

From the La Guinguette crossroads take the D342 back towards Moÿ. Just as you reach the outskirts of the town you will see a junction on the right. Turn sharply here and the cemetery is on the left. The British plot is at the top of the cemetery, marked by the flag pole. After the cavalry battle the wagons of 5/Cavalry Field Ambulance were quickly on the scene with their escort of lancers; under fire from German carbines, they recovered the wounded of both sides. In the cemetery you will find **Captain John Michell,** who has the epitaph 'He died at the head of his squadron' on his headstone. **Major Foster Swetenham** was killed early in the engagement by the wood at la Guinguette and **Privates Hugh Nolan** and **Charles Coote**, of C Squadron, 12/Lancers, were killed during the charge. 31 year old **Trumpet Major Edward Tompkins** died from the wounds to his thigh later in the day. The 20/Hussars lost only one man, 21 year old **Lance Corporal William Ryan,** who died from his wounds. Next to the 1914 casualties are two aircrew, casualties of November 1943, **Sergeant Frederick Wise** and 23 year old **Warrant Officer Alan Charlsworth**.

Stage 3 Tour

Puiseux-en-Retz Crossroads to the Marne

This forty mile tour begins on the northern edge of the Forêt de Retz, where the D811 and D250 meet at the crossroads 700 yards west of Puiseux-en-Retz **[1]**. The crossroads forms the centre of the position along which the Guards deployed early on 1 September. The majority of the 2nd Division had retired through Vivières on their way south, but 4 Guards Brigade had arrived at this point via Soucy and Puiseux. Once the orders to act as rearguard had been passed to **Brigadier General Robert Scott-Kerr**, 2/Coldstream Guards, under the command of **Lieutenant Colonel Cecil Pereira,** deployed along the edge of the forest towards Vivières, facing north. The right of the line – towards Puiseux – was the responsibility of 1/Irish Guards and their commanding officer, **Lieutenant Colonel the Hon George Morris**. It was through these two battalions, which were under the overall command of George Morris, that 2/Grenadier Guards and 3/Coldstream Guards marched before heading south on the D811 to reach the Rond de la Reine.

If you walk up the hill towards Soucy to the small agricultural layby on the right, you will be able to see the line of the forest along which Morris probably deployed his battalion. Colonel Morris – astride his horse – appeared to be everywhere at once. A man noted for his bravery and composure under fire, not half an hour before his death, after a period of sustained shellfire that had brought trees crashing down, he had called out to the men: 'D'you hear that? They're doing that to frighten you.' To which someone replied, 'If that's what they're after, they might as well stop. They succeeded with me hours ago.'

From the layby on the Soucy road you can get an idea of the ground covered by **Aubrey Herbert** when taking instructions from Colonel Morris to Cecil Pereira. After Morris had ordered 2/Coldstream to retire to a covering position along the railway line to the south, Pereira's line of retirement was through the forest to the west of the D811. Just as Morris and his Irish Guards were about to follow the Coldstream he received the orders to remain in position until 1.00pm to allow the division to stop for lunch! Unable to recall the Coldstream, he remained in position and it was this unfortunate order that was responsible for the desperate fighting rearguard through the forest and the heavy toll in casualties incurred by the battalion.

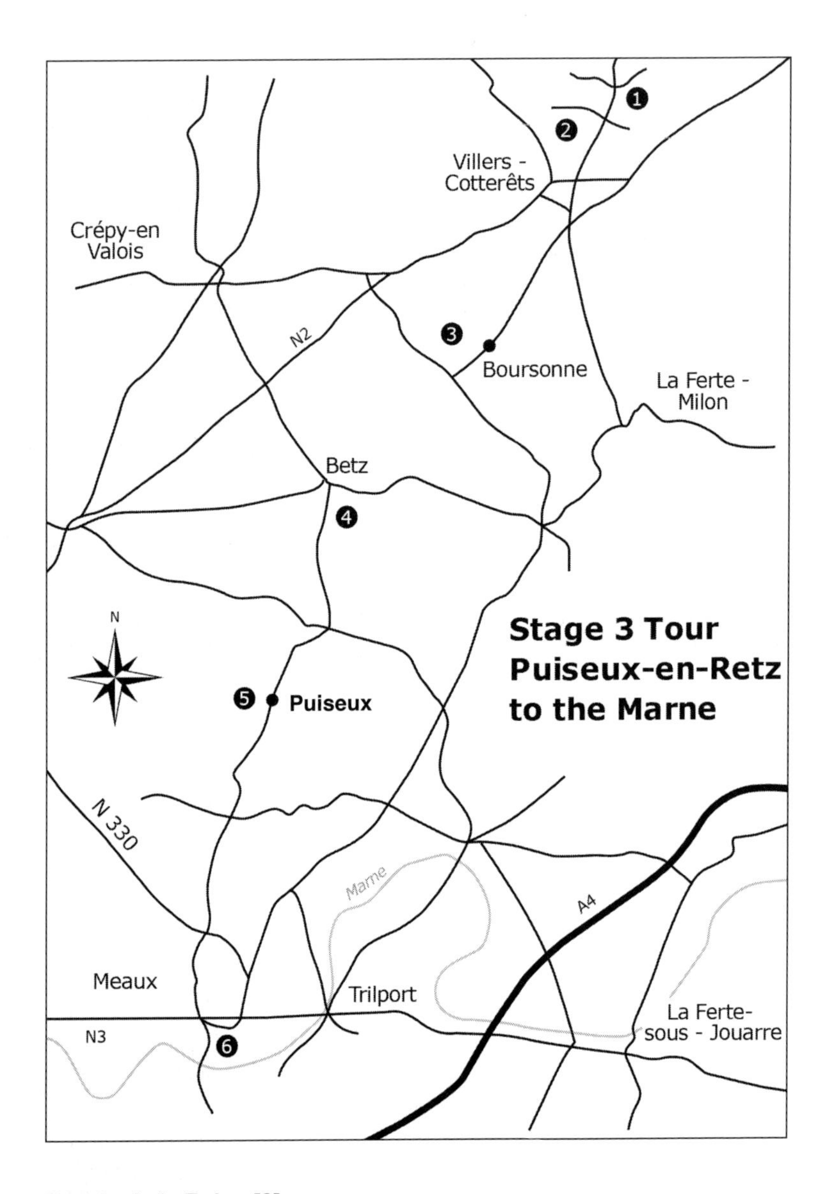

Ronde de la Reine [2]

Return to your vehicle and retrace your route back to the Ronde de la Reine. Travelling from this direction you can turn right at the forest crossroads along the minor road towards the Maison Forestière and park on the left. This forest road, running west – east through the forest, is the line along which 2/Grenadiers and 3/Coldstream positioned themselves after falling back from the crossroads west of Puiseux. Where you are

The Rond de la Reine crossroads north of Villers-Cotterêts.

now is the approximate position of the Grenadiers' battalion headquarters, while No. 4 Company was along the road to the west, past the Maison Forestière, where it was in touch with 3/Coldstream. Across the road to the east the Grenadiers' No 1 and 2 Companies were along the rising ground just south of the main ride which leads towards the **Mangin Memorial**.

As the Irish Guards fell back towards the Ronde de la Reine they passed through the lines of the Grenadiers and Coldstream. Colonel Morris had by this time been killed and the situation was becoming critical. At this point in the battle orders were given for a counter attack by two platoons from No. 4 Company, who were deployed near the Maison Forestière. In this attack **Second Lieutenant George Cecil** and **Lieutenant the Hon John Manners** were killed and a third officer, **Lieutenant Buddy Needham**, was wounded and taken prisoner. **Major George Jeffreys** would have been at battalion headquarters, which was at the crossroads, and it was probably here that he first saw the wounded Brigadier General Scott-Kerr and from where Lieutenant Colonel Corry took command of the brigade.

Lieutenant John Manners, whose body was never recovered.

The 3/Coldstream companies were forced to fall back towards the railway bridge diagonally behind the Grenadiers – a manoeuvre made all the more difficult by the dense undergrowth. **Major Bernard Gordon Lennox's** No. 2 Company, on the right of the line, gave covering fire before they too began filtering back towards the railway. It had been a very costly rearguard but without the professionalism and leadership by the brigade's senior officers and NCOs the casualty list would have been considerably longer. Certainly the withdrawal from the Rond de la Reine of the 2/Grenadiers was a masterly manoeuvre for which Major Jeffreys and the self discipline of all ranks deserve due credit.

The Guards Grave Cemetery

This is best approached on foot via the forest road leading down from the Maison Forestière. The cemetery is on the bend of the D81 and parking is practically impossible. Cross the road with care to the steps leading down to the cemetery, which was formed by the Irish Guards in November 1914 and contains ninety eight casualties, of whom twenty are unidentified. Of the guardsmen buried here, forty five are Grenadiers, twenty one are Irish Guards and eleven are from the Coldstream Guards. Only one man, **Private Mark Durkin** of 1/East Lancashire Regiment, was not a serving soldier in the Brigade of Guards. The youngest soldier is a 17 year old Grenadier Guardsman, **Lance Corporal Thomas Frederick Ayers**, and the oldest is 42 year old **Lieutenant Colonel the**

The Guards Grave Cemetery.

Hon George Henry Morris of the Irish Guards, who is buried side by side with **Second Lieutenant George Cecil** (2/Grenadier Guards), **Lieutenant Geoffrey Lambton** (2/Coldstream Guards) and **Major Charles Tisdsall** (1/Irish Guards). These four officers were eventually located and exhumed by George Morris' brother, Martin Henry Morris, 2nd Baron Killanin, in November 1914, after a previous attempt by Lady Violet Cecil to find her son's body had failed. Buried initially in a plot in the communal cemetery at Villers-Cotterêts, their remains were exhumed after the Armistice to be re-united with their men at Guards' Grave Cemetery. Killanin's party also found ninety four men, recorded their details where possible and reburied them in the grave which later became more formally known as the Guards Grave Cemetery. Cecil Morris embarked for France only days after his son Michael was born on 30 July 1914. Michael eventually succeeded his uncle at Baron Killanin in 1927 and after serving in the Second World War became the 6th President of the International Olympic committee in 1972. He died in 1999.

The Cecil Memorial

This imposing memorial is only a few metres from the Ronde de la Reine crossroads, on the right hand side of the road, and was commissioned in 1922 by Lady Violet Cecil in memory of her son, George Edward Cecil of the Grenadier Guards. The inscription on the back of the memorial reads: 'In Honour of the officers and men of the Grenadier, Coldstream and Irish Guards who fell near this spot on 1st September 1914. This memorial was placed here by the mother of one of them and is especially dedicated to

The Cecil Memorial

Second Lieutenant George Edward Cecil.' In 1978 the Grenadier Guards made arrangements for the memorial's future maintenance and transferred its upkeep to the CWGC.

The Mangin Memorial

Inaugurated in November 1926, the memorial commemorates the site of the Reaumont observatory tower erected on the orders of **General Charles Mangin** (1886–1925) at the time he commanded the French Tenth Army in July 1918. To reach the memorial, walk along the ride from the Ronde de la Reine past the lone memorial to **Lieutenant Henri de Chasseval** – a reminder that the Forêt de Retz played an important part in the Second Battle of the Marne in 1918 – until you are prompted by a signboard to leave the road and climb a small rise on the left, where you will find the memorial. To return to the Rond de la Reine either use the GR11A national footpath, which runs almost parallel to the ride you have just walked along, or retrace your steps. A map is useful.

Boursonne

We are now on the last leg of this tour and will follow the route taken by 4 Guards Brigade to Meaux and the Marne crossings. After leaving Villers-Cotterêts the 2nd Division headed south towards the Marne along the D81 to the village of Boursonne, where 2/Grenadier Guards was ordered to take up a position in the village to cover the withdrawal of 4 and 6 Brigades. Take the Avenue de Boursonne out of Villers-Cotterêts towards Boursonne. As the road emerges from the forest, a short distance north of the village of Boursonne, stop just after the cottage on the right. At 6.00pm on 1 September 1914 the Grenadier Guards' No. 3 Company was deployed astride the road between here and the northern outskirts of the village. **Captain Douglas Stephen** would have positioned his men as far as possible to cover the entrance to the village. We also know that **Major**

The forest line just to the north of Boursonne. It was from the forest on the left of the road that 6 Cavalry Brigade appeared and alarmed Major General Monro who at the time was in conversation with Major Jeffreys.

Boursonne - the 2nd Battalion Grenadier Guards would have marched down this road en route to Thury-en-Valois.

Jeffreys was here assessing the situation with **Major General Monro** and were discussing the fight to retrieve the 70/Battery guns. 'He stood (or rather sat on his horse) with us on the northerly outskirts of Boursonne', wrote Jeffreys in his diary. It was during this conversation that there was very nearly another case of friendly fire when, 'out of the forest about 500 or 600 yards away to our left front appeared some cavalry riding quickly along and apparently going to pass our left flank'. Monro yelled out to the Grenadiers to change front and open fire. 'I was almost certain they were British', wrote Jeffreys, who 'ordered the platoon to change front, but not to open fire, and got my glasses onto them when I at once saw the grey horses of the Scots Greys'. Gradually 6 Brigade filtered through the forest, passing the Grenadiers, until 2/Coldstream arrived, bringing up the rear. Jeffreys notes that his battalion fell in behind, 'as there appeared to be no orders and we had been forgotten by our own brigade'.

Continue into the village, where the Guards loopholed the garden walls and dug trenches in preparation for an attack. Jeffreys felt that, 'after two hours work we had a reasonably strong position' but, as had been the case on countless occasions before, orders arrived to abandon their positions and continue the march. To follow in the Grenadiers' footsteps continue through Boursonne – the road now becomes the D51 – and turn sharp left just before Ivors towards Autheuil-en-Valois on the D88. After approximately 3.5 kilometres, turn right on to the D18 towards Thury-en-Valois.

Thury-en-Valois

It was here that General Monro established his Divisional Headquarters when Major Jeffreys arrived with his Grenadiers he found that all the 4 Brigade supplies and transport were some four miles to the west at Betz. Apart from all the fighting in the forest, the battalion had covered some twenty three miles since 3.00am that morning and was exhausted. All the available accommodation had been taken up by 6 Brigade and there was nothing with which to provide a meal for the men. Jeffreys raised the roof and eventually demanded to see Monro, who made immediate arrangements for rations to be provided. A ration dump a mile outside the village, on the D77 towards Villeneuve-sous-Thury, provided the necessary bully beef, biscuit and jam:

> *Then the battalion just lay down by the road and slept. There was a farmhouse close by and (having issued orders that we would march at 2am to join the brigade) I and Stephen went in and groped our way into pitch dark room full of sleeping humanity of sorts and found a vacant corner and slept.*

Just before first light the next morning the battalion marched back to Thury. Jeffreys tells us they were reunited with the brigade at Betz before pressing on to Puisieux, where the battalion breakfasted.

The route down to the Marne now crosses some the Marne battlefields and memorials to that pivotal battle are very much in evidence. After you pass through Betz on the D332 a small French National Cemetery can be found on the right hand side. Larger monuments to the French dead can be seen at Barcy, where you will find the **Monument Notre-Dame de la Marne** on the D97. Also in evidence are the French and German cemeteries at Chambry and which are worthy of a visit. The German dead at Chambry are casualties of the Battle of the Ourq, while in the French cemetery 1,258 soldiers are remembered with the standard concrete cross – many of which are showing signs of wear.

Musée de la Grand Guerre at Meaux

From Barcy head south along the D38 towards Meaux and pick up the signs for the museum. If you are using a sat nav, the address is Route de Varreddes, which is off the D405. The museum was opened on 11 November 2011 and is housed in a slender, modernistic building designed by the French architect Christophe Lab. Outside is the huge 'American Monument', an ornately writhing figure of Liberty entwined

The Monument of Notre-Dame de la Marne.

The French National Cemetery at Chambry.

The Memorial to the Missing at La Ferté-sous-Jouarre.

with the dead and dying by sculptor Frederick Mac Monnies, which was unveiled in 1932 by the American Friends of France in the presence of French President Albert Lebrun to commemorate the First Battle of the Marne. The monument is sometimes referred to as the statue of 'tearful liberty'. Inside the museum there is plenty to interest the British and Commonwealth visitor and although the displays lean towards the French story of the Great War, the reconstructions of French and German trenches and the emphasis on the myriad collection of uniforms, equipment and weaponry worn and used by both sides is guaranteed to hold the interest of most.

The Memorial to the Missing of the Marne

I suggest after crossing the Marne at Meaux you head east along the N3 to La Ferté-sous-Jouarre to vist the memorial to the missing. The memorial was built on land given by **Adrien Fizeau**, former mayor of Jouarre, in memory of his father. The Fizeau connection is commemorated with bilingual inscriptions on either side of the steps leading up to the river-facing side of the memorial. Unveiled on 4 November 1928 by Sir William Pulteney, who commanded III Corps in 1914, the memorial commemorates the 3,740 officers and men of the BEF who fell at the battles of Mons, Le Cateau, the Marne and the Aisne between the end of August and early October 1914 and have no known graves. At the four corners of the pavement on which the monument stands are stone columns supporting urns that bear the coats of arms of

One of two identical Royal Engineers memorials that stand on the banks of the Marne commemorating the pontoon bridge built by 9 Field Company in September 1914.

the four constituent nations of the United Kingdom. The memorial was designed by **George Hartley Goldsmith**, a decorated veteran of the Western Front. For those of you wishing to view the register you will find that it is now kept at the Mairie and is only available for consultation during working hours.

The Royal Engineers Memorials
Although not technically part of the retreat, the two memorials are very much a part of the battlefield landscape at La Ferté. From the Memorial to the Missing, walk towards the river and under the road bridge. Ahead

The American Monument was inaugurated at a ceremony in the presence of President Albert Lebrun.

of you is the first of two identical obelisks marking the site of a pontoon bridge erected during the advance to the Aisne on 9/10 September 1914 by 9/Field Company, alongside the very bridge which 26/Field Company had destroyed a week earlier! Look across the river and you will see the second of the two memorials. The bridge was 218 feet long and was constructed mainly from material found locally.

Jardin du Lieutenant James Collingwood-Thompson

Behind the Memorial to the Missing is the garden dedicated to Edward James Vibart Collingwood-Thompson. Collingwood-Thompson was the first officer of 2/Royal Welch Fusiliers to be killed in action, an event that occurred nearby on 9 September, when he was fatally wounded during the battalion's advance towards the Aisne. A private memorial, which was

A permanent memorial to Lieutenant James Collingwood-Thompson.

Rozay-en-Brie – some twenty miles south of Meaux - marked the end of the retreat for many BEF units.

erected by his mother and which is notoriously difficult to locate, marks the exact spot where he was wounded and can be found some 250 yards further east. To find it is necessary to head down the Rue Fizeau/Quai des Anglais towards the river from the Memorial to the Missing – keeping the gardens on your left – until you reach the junction with the Rue des Carreaux on your right. Walk up this street to the junction with the Rue de Condé (D402) and you will see a cast metal plaque on the gable end of the last house on the right bearing the inscription in English and French. On the street corner below it there is also a small obelisk at ground level. Collingwood-Thompson is buried at Perreuse Château Franco-British Cemetery. The tour concludes here.

Appendix I

Approximate Daily March Statistics

	2nd Division I Corps	**3rd Division II Corps**	**4th Division III Corps after 31 August**
Date	**1st Battalion Gloucestershire Regiment**	**4th Battalion Middlesex Regiment**	**1st Battalion Somerset Light Infantry**
23 August	Not engaged at Mons	5 miles	Not engaged at Mons
24 August	17 miles	13 miles	Arrived Le Cateau 8 miles
25 August	15.5 miles	30 miles	6 miles
26 August	15 miles	30 miles Engaged at Le Cateau	3 miles Engaged at Le Cateau
27 August	23 miles	24 miles	12 miles
28 August	21 miles	17 miles	20 miles
29 August	rest	9 miles	11 miles
30 August	10 miles	16 miles	9 miles
31 August	18 miles	19 miles	15 miles
1 September	19 miles	16 miles	15 miles
2 September	18.5 miles	25 miles	9 miles
3 September	16.5 miles	11 miles	10 miles
4 September	11.5 miles	18 miles	9 miles
5 September	15 miles		20 miles
Total March Final destination	**203 miles Rozoy-en-Brie**	**233 miles Chevry- Cossigny**	**137 miles Briarde de Retal**

Appendix II

I Corps Order of Battle and German First and Second Army Order of Battle

Order of Battle of I Corps - August 1914

1st Division – General Officer Commanding - Major General S H Lomax

Brigades	Battalions	Artillery	Engineers	Field Ambulance
1 (Guards) Brigade *(Brig Gen F I Maxse)*	1/Coldstream *(Lt Col J Ponsonby)* 1/Scots Guards *(Lt Col H C Lowther)* 1/Black Watch *(Lt Col A Grant-Duff)* 2/Munster Fusiliers *(Major P Charrier)*	XXV Brigade (113, 114, 115 Btys) XXVI Brigade (116, 117, 118 Btys) XXXIX Brigade (46, 51, 54 Btys) XLIII Howitzer Brigade (30, 40, 57 Btys) 26 Heavy Bty RGA In addition to the individual brigade ammunition columns and 26 Heavy Battery Ammunition Column, the divisional artillery was supported by the 1st Divisional Ammunition Column.	23 Field Company *(Maj C Russell-Brown)* 26 Field Company *(Maj H L Pritchard)* 1st Signal Company	1 Field Ambulance 2 Field Ambulance 3 Field Ambulance *(Lt Col G Cree)*
2 Infantry Brigade *(Brig Gen E S Bulfin)*	2/Royal Sussex Regiment *(Lt Col E H Montresor)* 1/Loyal North Lancs *(Lt Col G C Knight)* 1/Northamptonshire Regiment *(Lt Col E Osborne Smith)* 2/King's Royal Rifle Corps *(Lt Col E Pearce-Serocold)*		Divisional Mounted Troops A Squadron 15/(The King's) Hussars *(Capt O B Walker)* 1/Cyclist Company	
3 Infantry Brigade *(Brig Gen H S Landon)*	1/Queen's Royal West Surrey *(Lt Col D Warren)* 1/South Wales Borderers *(Lt Col H E B Leach)* 1/Gloucestershire Regiment *(Lt Col A C Lovett)* 2/Welch Regiment *(Lt Col B Morland)*			

2nd Division – General Officer Commanding – Major General C C Monro

Brigades	Battalions	Artillery	Engineers	Field Ambulance
4 (Guards) Brigade *(Brig Gen R Scot-Kerr)*	2/Grenadier Guards *(Lt Col N A Corry)* 2/Coldstream Guards *(Lt Col C E Pereira)* 3/Coldstream Guards *(Lt Col G P Fielding)* 1/Irish Guards *(Lt Col Hon G Morris)*	XXXIV Brigade (22, 50, 70 Btys) XXXVI Brigade (15, 48, 71 Btys) XLI Brigade (9, 16, 17 Btys) XLIV Howitzer Brigade (47, 56, 60 Btys) 35 Heavy Bty RGA In addition to the individual brigade ammunition columns and 35 Heavy Battery Ammunition Column, the divisional artillery was supported by the 2nd Divisional Ammunition Column.	5 Field Company *(Maj C N North)* 11 Field Company *(Maj P Denis de Vitre)*	4 Field Ambulance 5 Field Ambulance 6 Field Ambulance
5 Infantry Brigade *(Brig Gen R C Haking)*	2/Worcestershire Regiment *(Lt Col C B Westmacott)* 2/Ox and Bucks Light Infantry *(Lt Col H R Davies)* 2/Highland Light Infantry *(Lt Col A A Wolfe-Murray)* 2/Connaught Rangers *(Lt Col A W Abercrombie)*		Divisional Mounted Troops B Squadron 15/(The King's) Hussars *(Capt Hon W A Nugent)* 2/Cyclist Company	
6 Infantry Brigade *(Brig Gen R H Davies)*	1/King's Liverpool Regiment *(Lt Col W S Bannatyne)* 2/South Staffordshire Regiment *(Lt Col C S Davidson)* 1/ Royal Berkshire Regiment *(Lt Col M D Graham)* 1/King's Royal Rifle Corps *(Lt Col E Northy)*			

5 Cavalry Brigade *(Brig Gen Sir P W Chetwode)*	2/Dragoons (Royal Scots Greys) *(Lt Col C B Bulkeley-Johnston)* 12/(Prince of Wales' Own) Lancers *(Lt Col F Wormald)* 20/Hussars *(Lt Col G T Edwards)*	J Battery RHA and Ammunition Column	4 Field Troop 5 Signal Troop	5 Cavalry FA

Imperial German Army – Order of Battle August 1914

(units referred to in the text)

First Army – Generalobest Alexander von Kluck

II Corps	*von Linsingen*	3rd and 4th Divisions
III Corps	*von Lochow*	5th and 6th Divisions
IV Corps	*Sixt von Armin*	7th and 8th Divisions
IX Corps	*von Quast*	17th and 18th Divisions
III Reserve Corps	*von Beseler*	5th Reserve and 6th Reserve Divisions
IV Reserve Corps	*von Gronau*	7th Reserve and 22nd Reserve Divisions
IX Reserve Corps	*von Boehn*	17th Reserve and 18th Reserve Divisions
10th,11th and 27th Landwehr Brigade		

Second Army – Generalobest Karl von Bülow

Guard Corps	von Plettenberg	1st Guard and 2nd Guard Divisions
VII Corps	von Einem	13th and 14th Divisions
X Corps	Von Emmich	19th and 20th Divisions
Guard Reserve Corps	von Gallwitz	3rd Guard and 1st Guard Reserve Divisions
VII Reserve Corps	von Zwehl	13th and 14th Reserve Divisions
X Reserve Corps	Graf von Kirchbach	2nd Guard Reserve and 14th Guard Reserve Divisions
25th and 29th Landwehr Brigades		

Second Cavalry Corps – Lieutenant General von der Marwitz

2nd, 4th, 9th Cavalry Divisions	3rd, 4th 7th 9th 10th Jager Battalions

Select Bibliography

Ascoli, D, *The Mons Star*, Harrap 1981

Carnock, Lord, *The History of the 15th The King's Hussars 1914-1922*, Crypt House Press 1932.

Craster, J, *Fifteen Rounds a Minute*, Macmillan 1976.

Darling, J C, *20th Hussars in the Great War*, Privately published 1923.

Edmonds, J E, *Military Operations France and Belgium 1914*, Volume 1, Macmillan 1926.

Gardner, N, *Trial by Fire*, Praeger 2003.

Gliddon, G, *VCs Handbook*, Sutton 2005.

Hamilton, Lord E, *The First Seven Divisions*, Hurst & Blackett 1916.

McCance, Captain S, *History of The Royal Munster Fusiliers from 1861 to 1922*, Aldershot 1927.

Murland, J, *Retreat and Rearguard 1914*, Pen and Sword Books 2011.

O'Rourke, B G, *In the Hands of the Enemy*, Longmans, Green and Co 1915.

Ponsonby, F, *The Grenadier Guards In The Great War of 1914-1918*, Macmillan 1920.

Posek, von M, *The German Cavalry 1914 in Belgium and France*, Naval & Military Press 2007.

Prichard, H L, (Editor) *History of The Corps of Royal Engineers (Volume 5)*, Institute of Royal Engineers 1951.

Ross of Bladensburg, Sir J, *The Coldstream Guards 1914-1918*, Oxford University Press 1928.

Sheffield, G & Bourne, J, *Douglas Haig War Diaries and Letters 1914-1918*, Orion 2005.

Spears, Sir E, *Liaison 1914*, Eyre & Spottiswoode 1930.

Terraine J. *Mons, Retreat to Victory*, Wordsworth 2002.

Wyrall, E, *The Gloucestershire Regiment in the War 1914-1918*, Methuen 1931.

Unpublished sources

The National Archives

Unit War Diaries in WO 95

Service Records in WO 339

Personal papers in WO 106 and CAB 45

Prisoner of War Reports in WO 161

Index